The Executive's Guide to Supply Management Strategies

The Executive's Guide to Supply Management Strategies

Building Supply Chain Thinking Into All Business Processes

David A. Riggs
Sharon L. Robbins

AMACOM
American Management Association
New York • Atlanta • Boston • Chicago • Kansas City • San Francisco • Washington, D.C.
Brussels • Mexico City • Tokyo • Toronto

Library of Congress Cataloging-in-Publication Date

Riggs, David A.
  The executive's guide to supply management strategies : building
supply chain thinking into all business processes / David A. Riggs,
Sharon L. Robbins.
    p.   cm.
  Includes index.
  ISBN 0–8144–0385–9
  1. Industrial procurement—Management.   I. Robbins, Sharon L.
II. Title.
  HD39.5.R54   1997
  658.7'2—dc21   97–35490
                                                                      CIP

Printing number

10   9   8   7   6   5   4   3

Contents

Preface

Volumes have been written recently about the ever-increasing competitive pressures facing CEOs around the globe, and the dramatic decreasing of cycle times to bring innovative solutions to satisfy customers' needs and wants, all within a framework of withering cost cutting that reduces internal resources available to respond.

Companies seemingly marshall every resource to meet these demands. CEOs understand exactly how to focus the marketing group, how to motivate sales, and apply the best people to engineering and manufacturing techniques and equipment. But there's often uncertainty about the role and opportunity suppliers to these companies present. The usual first reaction is simple leverage to the maximum extent possible to squeeze every dime—to show no mercy. Apply the not-so-golden rule: "Do exactly to them as our customers do to us." Not only does this fail to produce a low total cost of ownership, but misses significant strategic potential.

In the past two years, we have read in national publications about enlightened companies who believe that the way they buy, the way they align themselves with their supply base, and the people and the strategies those people apply are truly effective. Still, most stop short of realizing the full potential available for the asking. Efforts are inconsistent, strategies are incomplete, and coordination between senior management and the rest of the organization is spotty at best. This is true of service and manufacturing businesses alike.

This book succinctly defines a process for companies to realize competitive advantage through reduced costs, cycle time innovation, and eliminating non-value-adding work by a managed and measured process to maximize the use of supplier resources to create real value and to drive business focus on its own core competencies.

But even more important, it outlines a specific "how-to" that not only defines roles and actions, but *gives the CEO measurements* to monitor progress. The result is a three-tier process:

The first is a market and evaluation process to determine best suppliers, meet the company's cost and quality objectives, and to consolidate the supply base.

The second identifies opportunities for optimizing materials and service flow and usage, resulting in reduced total cost of ownership and eliminating non-value-adding work.

The third evolution focuses on how change in process, product, or technology can provide breakthrough competitive advantage.

This is all about solutions—about structured, commonsense answers that are implementable and measurable—that not only provide specific recipes to the organization's procurement professionals, but the strategy and step-by-step measurements for the CEO to realize benefits immediately and sustainably.

David A. Riggs
Sharon L. Robbins

The Executive's Guide to Supply Management Strategies

CHAPTER 1

Introduction

There is nothing more difficult to take in hand, more perilous to conduct, or more uncertain in its success, than to take the lead in the introduction of a new order of things.

—Niccolò Machiavelli, *The Prince*

It does not take much strength to do things, but it requires great strength to decide what to do.

—Elbert Hubbard, "A Message to Garcia"

The preceding observations are both profound and appropriate to the subject of this book. Our objectives in writing this book are both to remove the peril and uncertainty in the new supply management order and to provide you with the strength, through knowledge and step-by-step processes, to decide exactly what to do to allow your business to realize the wealth of benefits afforded by supply management.

We have written this book to provide upper-level management—executive management, senior management, chief executive officers—with an understanding of the concept and benefits of supply management, the means needed to realize and measure those benefits, and the support and guidance required to implement supply management, right down to the questions to ask leading up to and following the implementation process. *The Executive's Guide to Supply Management Strategies* is aimed squarely at the level of management that is most cognizant of the increasing need to stretch resources and simultaneously provide competitive advantage to ensure success into the next century. These are the men and women who are positioned to shape the future and create the environment to allow their organizations to flourish. At the same time, the book is entirely appropriate for procurement leaders and professionals as well as for functional and cross-functional leaders, all of whom need a road map to keep sight of their multiple corporate objectives via use of a new process.

Much has been written about different types of initiatives and structures for improving business results, and many of these ideas have been tried. With varying degrees of commitment and success, would-be innovators have become a little jaded and confused, and with each new twist move from euphoria to "This, too, shall pass."

Likewise, many procurement philosophies, ranging from "Just get it here!" to intense leveraging for price, from harsh adversarial relationships to fuzzy, feel-good partnerships, have left procurement professionals unsure of their roles. Nonetheless, an awakening to the importance of the procurement role is evident everywhere.

It is evident, too, that many senior management groups have been uncertain of the role that procurement professionals should play and the capabilities they must have for the changing demands made of them. Even more evident is the short list of companies utilizing their supplier base successfully as a strategic extension of their own research and development, manufacturing, and even marketing departments.

What seems to be lacking in this endeavor is a way to consistently use supply resources to improve overall business performance. This linkage does not require a fundamental change in corporate objectives and measurements, but draws more explicitly on external resources to create competitive advantage.

Many companies are "getting it." Others are only partially getting it. Most are operating much as they always have with some upgrading of the purchasing staff or elevating of their reporting level. They are often effectively leveraging their pricing with suppliers without realizing: (1) the greater benefits of total cost or shorter cycle time, (2) the impact of better quality, or (3) the utilization of supplier expertise. More are realizing some of the benefits of strategic suppliers and their capabilities, but lack the necessary link to their own business goals and measurements.

From "Purchasing's New Muscle" in the February 20, 1995, issue of *Fortune* comes this headline: "What used to be a corporate backwater is becoming a fast-track job as purchasers show they can add millions to the bottom line." It goes on to add perspective:

> Simple Fact: When the goal is boosting profits by dramatically lowering costs, a business should look first to what it buys. On average, manufacturers shell out 55 cents of each dollar of revenue on goods and services, from raw materials to overnight mail.
>
> By contrast, labor seldom exceeds 6% of sales, overhead 3%. So purchasing exerts far greater leverage on earnings than anything else. By shrinking the bill 5%, a typical manufacturer adds almost 3% to net profits. Extracting that much from labor would mean chopping the entire pay-

roll in half. The same arithmetic applies to service businesses: at Merrill Lynch and Solomon Brothers, for example, purchases of good and services account for more than 15% of revenues.*

The article goes on to point out that many companies, including AT&T and Chrysler, have the broader goal of going beyond simply lowering price to lowering the total cost of each part or service they buy by developing supply relationships that extend beyond short-term contracts. This fosters continual improvement, bit by bit, in areas such as standardization and driving out waste.

Some companies are realizing still more benefits by simplifying the acquisition process—reducing paperwork, implementing more electronic ordering, using paperless just-in-time inventory demand release systems, and the like.

Not enough organizations, however, use the real expertise of their suppliers, those companies in the business of processing silicon wafers or overnighting packages or manufacturing specialty pumps. Core competencies are those skills that exemplify an organization's true expertise. Just as it is important to understand your own core competencies, it is equally important to supplement them with the core competencies of your suppliers, who should be the best available. If you're dealing with the best, they *should* know more about that field than you and be able to provide expertise if you listen.

Tapping into this expertise is what *supply management* is all about: the process of examining all facets of the buying and actual use of purchased materials and services and

*Shawn Tully, "Purchasing's New Muscle," Fortune (February 20, 1995), pp. 75–83. Reprinted with permission. Copyright © 1995 Time, Inc. All rights reserved.

linking the resources of leading suppliers to the strategic goals of your company, thus strengthening its competitive advantage in the marketplace.

Supply management applies equally to manufacturing and service businesses and to the products and services purchased by each.

We have seen the trend. The logic is compelling. The benefits are understood. Parts of the concept are everywhere. What's missing is implementation. What this book is about is implementation with a clear understanding of what is required to get there from here and a methodology to do it—and to do it without dismembering the corporation for yet another guru-driven initiative. We are talking basics—and they fit within the normal corporate planning and operations structure.

Rather, it is a disciplined, systematic improvement process. By applying it to your company's purchase of materials, supplies, and services, you can expose opportunity and improve your company's performance and competitive position. Supply management, by providing access to leading industry practices, improving cost and value relationships, streamlining internal and external procedures, and reducing your time-to-market cycle, will allow your company to deliver superior, unique value to the market at the lowest prices possible.

IMPLEMENTATION GUIDE

[Implementation Guides conclude each chapter. They contain key ideas or questions to ask yourself and the others around you engaged in this process, suggesting implementation steps appropriate to each chapter.]

Remember, this is not a newly invented idea. It is a

leading-edge idea that is partially understood and already implemented piecemeal in a number of companies. This book is about how to pull it all together and, more crucial, implement it—the single factor that will determine which businesses and business leaders will distinguish themselves from their competitiors.

CHAPTER 2

Let's Stop "Admiring" the Supply Problem

Everyone we've met during the last several years claims to be involved with supply management in some shape or form. We've heard it called procurement reengineering, supplier relationship initiatives, strategic supply side management (as though the addition of the word *strategic* alone somehow elevates its importance), and supplier alliance teams. Need we continue?

If the creativity in naming this field had been directed toward solving, rather than "admiring," the problem, the task of problem analysis would have been completed long ago and effective supply management programs would now be the norm. But instead, legions of Fortune 500 personnel have now examined every facet of what's wrong with the way a business purchases—without finding a *comprehensive,* action-oriented solution. The rewards for admiring problems must obviously be greater than for solving them.

This is where you come in, because without executive leadership, people will "admire" until time runs out.

Now, let us be clear. If you and your business have all the time in the world, no profit pressures, and ample competitive advantage, you don't need to look to the supply side of your business for new opportunity. However, if you are among those executives who are continually challenged to produce to new heights, this forgotten cost center may have some jewels that you have overlooked.

What Do You Know About This Overlooked Cost Center?

First off, do you know how much your company spends for all of its purchased materials and services? Why not admit it, you probably don't have a sweet clue, let alone know how it's spent or among how many suppliers. And you can be thankful it's too early in the book to ask the really hard question, "How do you know that you're getting your money's worth?" That we can't even venture a guess is symptomatic of the basic problem: Nobody cares!

Let's go back to managing what we know—marketing, sales, manufacturing, downsizing, cutting budgets, quality processes, team building . . . these alone can occupy us for the rest of our lives. So why examine purchasing at all?

Very simply, your business is spending, conservatively, 25 to 40 percent of every sales dollar on purchased materials and services. These are net cash dollars out of pocket. The total costs for these purchases, including hidden payroll costs, waste and misuse, processing costs, and inventories, bring the actual cash impact to almost twice the purchase cost alone.

How could any area of expenditure be so large and so forgotten? Very simply, it was buried by lack of interest and other priorities, and has stayed hidden, out of sight, since centralized procurement began more than fifty years ago.

Early Centralized Structures for Purchasing

The need for acquiring supporting goods and services is almost coincidental with the formation of business. Only the earliest farmer could boast of total self-sufficiency, called vertical integration in today's world.

At first, businesses acquired the goods and services required to make or deliver their products in an ad hoc manner. However, by the 1930s, Adam Smith's division of labor theories had created a new way of organizing work by task in order to increase a worker's efficiency. Aggregating like work tasks into one organizational unit created economies of skill and supervision. These, in turn, created functional organization structures still in existence today.

The Functional Department

From these beginnings, the earliest purchasing or procurement department, which performed the functional work of acquiring the goods and services needed to make a company's product, was conceived. This new centralized function was created to increase efficiencies in three areas of business needs:

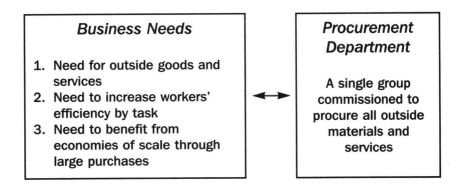

Business Needs	*Procurement Department*
1. Need for outside goods and services 2. Need to increase workers' efficiency by task 3. Need to benefit from economies of scale through large purchases	A single group commissioned to procure all outside materials and services

The functional procurement department was centralized within a business and empowered one set of people to perform the tasks of purchasing, which were to:

- Produce purchase orders.
- Plan and receive materials.
- Select suppliers.
- Schedule material/service use.
- Negotiate terms.
- Pay bills.
- Develop contracts.
- Monitor inventory.

From the 1930s through the 1970s, this centralized function worked well. Businesses gained leverage in their purchasing and efficiencies from standardized practices in the transactional process of buying, receiving, and paying bills.

However, the 1970s marked the beginning of a whole new era of organizational concepts:

1. The advent of the individual
2. The power of teams

These two concepts directly challenged virtually every centralized functional organization in a business, including accounting, personnel, information services, and many more.

Now, increasing numbers of individuals and teams began to make specific demands on these centralized structures originally designed to process large volumes of standard transactions, resulting in processing errors, increased transaction time, increased handoffs as work moved from one functional group to another, and increased budget expense. These, in turn, created the need to add dedicated people to supply functional support to individual businesses, resulting in added management infrastructure and staffing costs. In short, superimposing these *new* concepts on *old* structures made organizations unwieldy.

Proliferation of Suppliers and Transactions

As individuals began specifying more and more suppliers, purchasing departments were left with the primary responsibility of only processing orders. The new internal focus on satisfying the individual or team need has resulted in a wave of purchasing practices that do not conform to the original intent of a common centralized function. What remain are administrative tasks of purchasing paperwork. There is little opportunity to affect the purchase decision, the supplier selection, the buying process, or the evaluation of results or the opportunity to leverage the actual purchase based on the company's need to satisfy an external customer. In short, purchasing has become a non-value-adding administrative task in far too many businesses.

As a result, the majority of businesses now face the following problems:

■ A proliferation of suppliers, certainly more than 1,000 and in some businesses 10,000 or more.

■ An explosion in non-value-adding transactions, most of these for $1,000 or less, in purchased materials or services, resulting in little time spent on the strategic purchases opportunities of the supply side.

■ Material and service variability, with multiple suppliers delivering their version of the same specifications.

■ No opportunity to create leverage from a single purchase order because of minimum economies of scale from multiple suppliers. In addition, the small order rarely commands the attention of the supplier's senior management and virtually never enjoys the benefits of supplier's innovation in product or process improvements.

■ Purchasing has become a transactional business function with no one managing or leading the "business process" of acquiring materials and services. It's all purchase orders and payments with little time for supply strategy.

These problems have resulted in hidden costs that are "marbleized" throughout an organization and its P&L. The purchasing expenditures, generally consuming between 40 and 60 percent of total revenue, are divided into thousands of small transactions, driven by individual or team requirements, and executed at the transactional level with no value added to the business's customer and at the same time adding to indirect costs.

The results:

■ *Noncompetitive costs* for these expenditures
■ *High transaction costs,* on average $152 to process a purchase order, the majority of which are for goods under $1,000
■ *Non-value-adding work,* for example, administrative work for purchasing, receiving, and accounts payable clerks, auditors, secretaries, attorneys, supervisors—all involved in sequential, duplicative tasks
■ "Shadow" workforce time, employees, including management, spending sizable amounts of time making purchasing decisions (all too often about materials and services that have nothing to do with the core competency of the business), time that

could be otherwise devoted to improving the business's competitive advantage

What's wrong with this picture? Very simply, the process is broken, and the goal of maximizing the value of dollars spent is long forgotten.

Administrative vs. Managing Processes

In today's competitive marketplace, where every business is striving to reduce its cost of delivering more distinctive products and services to its customers, a business can no longer ignore the importance of the procurement function and its access to new market potential. The most obvious change to be made is to replace the traditional burdensome administrative process with a simple managing process that creates value with each purchase. The supply management process brings simple concepts and tools to revaluing a business's total purchasing behavior. The process is too simple to implement to justify trying to fix a traditional administrative system. In short, get out a clean sheet of paper and begin asking, "What are we trying to do here?"

The Situation Analysis Result . . . for the Last Time, Ever

The simple truth that there is nothing worth saving in the traditional procurement process or structure is too painful for some to accept. So we are continually hearing of new procurement redesign efforts beginning with a new situation analysis—yet another reexamination of the current process, as though it is really expected to identify the symptoms and diagnose the problem in a new way.

Figure 2-1 shows the inevitable outcomes. The only change necessary is to fill in the business name.

Figure 2-2 summarizes how various groups of people spend time as they engage the current procurement process.

Figures 2-1 and 2-2 summarize the more salient results we typically find in each business as it first begins to reexamine its procurement process. As these results are compiled, a compelling picture of the need for drastic change emerges:

- Noncompetitive costs, often 5–10 percent behind the industry leader
- Lengthy cycle times for purchases
- Long cycle times to implement improvements
- Shadow workforce (people other than procurement professionals) performing a wide variety of indirect purchasing functions and possessing varied skill levels, diminishing market leverage
- Lack of synergy in purchases among business locations
- Lack of synergy among locations to achieve benefits of best practices
- No opportunity for focused innovation
- Purchasing personnel with direct marketing knowledge are often excluded from important purchased services and goods arenas
- No opportunity to link key suppliers with key customers to pursue new product or service opportunities

Finally, the saddest result of all is that the only individual within an organization who knows anything at all about the actual purchased supply or purchased service is the buyer. Yet the buyer has almost no time to think about

Figure 2-1. Typical situation analysis results.

---

*Annual Business Spending for Purchases of Materials
and Services*
    Manufacturing business   50–60% of total revenues
    Service business   15–25% of total revenues

Total Cost of Ownership
    Tangible products (equipment, chemicals, office supplies)
    Purchase cost = 35–50% of total cost

    Intangible services (professional consulting, contract labor)
    Purchase cost = 60–85% of total cost

    Difference between purchase cost and total cost of ownership
    includes cash and noncash impacts, such as payroll time,
    inventory, processing costs, waste, and misuse.

Number of Suppliers
Organization size (by revenue)	< $1 billion	1,000–5,000 suppliers
	$1–5 billion	6,000–20,000 suppliers
	$5–15 billion	20,000–40,000 suppliers

    Average purchase will involve 7 to 10 suppliers
    High supplier response: 30
    Low supplier response: 01

Transactional Analysis
    10% of all purchase orders account for 90% of all spending.
    80% of all purchase orders are for $2,000 or less.
    Most approval policies require executive signatures for
    purchases over $500.

Purchase/Payable Process Description
    Transactional process utilizing purchase orders, invoices, check
    requests, and matching purchase orders/invoices and receiving
    documents to release supplier payment. This same process is used
    for virtually all purchases, regardless of importance to the business
    or the dollar size.

Figure 2-2. Typical management task analysis results.

Procurement Professionals
- Time is spent almost exclusively in buying, processing, and handling delivery logistics.
- No time is spent managing use or implementing best practices.
- Minimal time is spent measuring performance and providing supplier feedback.
- Negligible time is spent redesigning the supply flow and usage, including streamlined ordering and supplier payment methods.

Operating Personnel/Internal Requisitioners
- Spend majority of time specifying choices and approving purchases.
- No time is spent in comprehensive market reviews or best-cost or best-practice benchmarking.
- Minimal time is spent in supplier cost analysis.
- No time is spent in creating a strategy to manage or optimize use.
- No time is spent in evaluating performance.

Executive Management
- No mechanisms exist to permit periodic reviews of purchase effectiveness by type of supply.
- No vehicles exist within current planning processes to target or measure procurement practices improvement.
- Virtually no time is spent, other than during annual budget preparation, seeking new supply strategies or sharing benchmark learning.

Technology
- Expenditure data not available.
- Inadequate to automate simplified transaction process.

the entire supply chain: the incoming material or service and its actual use. By never focusing on this supply chain, the business voluntarily forfeits any benefits the marketplace may offer in improved functionality or improve-

ments in cost. Sad to say, for purchased materials and services consume such large portions of business revenues.

It is high time to stop "admiring" this problem. The
reasons for the problems are clear but irrelevant to the need
for fast improvements in value for every dollar spent.
However, the path forward requires executive leadership
to shape new direction because the required changes entail
shifts in organizational processes, systems, and structures.
Mere mortals can't handle this.

IMPLEMENTATION GUIDE

How to know whether your business is still "admiring" the
problem:

1. Are you actively engaged in defining/understanding a
   new management process to create purchased
   supply strategies?

For all materials and services?	Yes	No
For some materials and services?	Yes	No

2. Which measures have you selected to evaluate
   performance?

Pricing histories?	Yes	No
Cash flow tracking?	Yes	No
Cost by supply stream?	Yes	No
Total cost/supply stream/year?	Yes	No

3. Are your procurement professionals consolidating
   your supplier base?

Yes	No

Has significant change been made during the last
year . . .

50% reduction?	Yes	No
25% reduction?	Yes	No
5% reduction?	Yes	No

4. Have you streamlined your procurement process,
   including new policies, methods, and information
   technologies?

   Yes   No

5. Are senior financial and procurement executives
   actively involved in procurement reengineering or
   supplier consolidation/supplier relationship
   programs?

   Yes   No

6. Can you describe specific benefits or outcomes that
   have resulted in the last year?

   Yes   No

Score 5 points for every "no" response. If you have 25
points or higher, your organization is definitely "admiring," not
implementing.

We know from experience that correctly redesigning procurement processes will produce *tangible cash benefits
quickly.* So if you cannot articulate hard results in improving
profitability and management practices, your peers and sub-
ordinates are waiting for leadership to set the tone, remove
barriers, and provide permission for change.

Select 1 or 2:

1. You now see a case for executive leadership in supply management but don't yet know enough to provide direction.	→	Continue to read. (We'll tell you how.)
2. You think you are already redesigning your supply management approach, with tangible results.	→	Read only the Implementation Guides to check your course of direction.

CHAPTER 3

A Brief History of Procurement Initiatives —Just Not Enough

In what could be called a field dash toward procurement enlightenment, the 1980s brought us to a rediscovery of market *leverage*—the wholesale gathering of requirements and specifications, generally for production materials required by manufacturing businesses. Annual bidding events involving every company in the Free World spawned rooms of suppliers at bidders' conferences. Requests for Proposal (RFPs) went to all in a winner-take-all competition for the business's requirements, sometimes to be awarded instantly on a small commodity grouping, sometimes on larger groupings with subsequent best-and-final negotiations. The objective was price, and lower prices resulted. There were substantial cost savings, so the process was passed down the chain. Broader product and service categories and cross categories were exercised. Many companies turned these adventures into a draconian art form. And the prices kept dropping. Sometimes the winning suppliers dropped as well, but there were always more where those came from. Customer clout, volume, and leverage ruled, benefits flowed to the large, and the principle became *might equals right.*

The good news was that this approach attracted a lot of senior management attention. José Ignacio López De Arriortúa, head of General Motors Purchasing in the early 1990s, was probably the most widely recognized proponent of leverage—aggregation of volume, relentless bidding competition, and price focus. These produced benefits to the General Motors bottom line, but the results were all too often short-lived.

The other good news was that companies began to trim their supply base, limiting the number of suppliers they had to deal with. Companies did have the opportunity to manage those suppliers more effectively and even started to "reengineer" some procurement processes. Some established umbrella contracts that allowed users to release against them, eliminating the cumbersome issuance of individual purchase orders. Systems solutions provided easier release and tracking mechanisms as well. Procurement cards were used for low-dollar-value purchases, again freeing buyer time to allow the buyer to do other, more value-added tasks. A common offshoot, however, was the misconception that this was now an opportunity to downsize procurement operations.

Problems With the Early Initiatives

Looking back, we see some flaws, some opportunities missed in these early efforts to fix procurement. As GM and others learned in the post-Lopez era, the benefits from leveraging and the fractured reengineering efforts were transitory. Supplier trust and responsiveness were damaged. Relationships were frayed, good ideas were lost, and technical and creative capabilities were falling victim to a one-dimensional process.

Significant gaps were apparent. There was only a short-term cash focus. Attention was paid only to price or best acquisition costs, failing to include some of the hidden costs of the procurement activity itself.

Some companies paid attention to inventory costs, but they often failed to account for more than the cost of money: Obsolescence, loss, handling, and the like were often overlooked, although transportation might sometimes be adequately considered. The real cost considerations for the way we actually use products and services were rarely considered, especially if the costs were for indirect or professional labor. There was simply no focus on how best to use products or services in order to gain the most value, or to eliminate wasted steps or mistakes. Often there were better solutions, which the right supply market analysis could have uncovered or which could have been developed if the pertinent information had been exchanged at the right levels of the supplier and using organizations or if the right links with supply R&D or manufacturing groups had been in place. Quality variables were very often overlooked or not adequately accounted for in the cost of quality analyses. The very real costs in time and effort expended from the very first realization of a need until that need is satisfied and value is received were not adequately mapped, identified, or accounted for as a total cost consideration in the procurement and use of goods and services.

In typical procurements that focus on the buying process and leverage alone, the value of reduced cycle time was underrealized or not realized at all. The time-to-market cycle (the time from product or service inception until market introduction) is of tremendous strategic importance, yet was often not considered part of procurement strategy. Also, the positive impact on cash flow provided by having a simple process to guide the transition from need to fulfillment was often overlooked in the procurement process and in the overall business development process.

All too slowly many companies began to realize that a satisfactory process to focus and actually manage their purchased production materials, supplies, and services (including those expenditures not traditionally thought of as purchasing opportunities or necessarily bought by purchasing professionals) simply did not exist. And so, even with these initial leveraging and procurement transaction reengineering efforts, companies had not consciously developed, much less put in place, streamlined, consistent, further-reaching processes that would provide focus and lead to the creation of new value.

Reducing the number of suppliers from thousands to hundreds generates economies of scale by leveraging purchase volume among fewer suppliers. Certainly, immediate dollar savings accrue from these lower prices. However, if a company can reduce suppliers *and* redesign the buying and paying process, many costly transactions can be eliminated or replaced with more efficient electronic solutions, including fax-ordering and credit card purchases. Effective process redesign frees up procurement time to focus on more value-adding work, such as market analyses, cost-modeling, and benchmarking best-usage practice.

Figure 3-1 indicates that 90 percent of a typical purchasing organization's time is spent on purchase orders that account for only 10 percent of total dollar expenditures. The majority of procurement and payables time is consumed by processing these low-value purchase transactions. In most companies today:

Figure 3-1. Annual purchase order analysis.

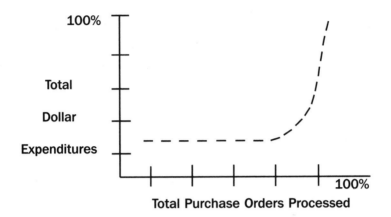

- Few processes exist to manage the larger dollar purchases.
- No process exists to manage the small and fragmented purchases.

Many eager procurement and business leaders began to recognize the need to reduce the number of suppliers and consolidate the supplier base and to simplify transactions. They stopped short, however, of pursuing the full benefit that comes from developing strategies that maximize the value of the entire sourced material or service supply stream, shown in Figure 3-2.

Procurement traditionally deals primarily only with the shaded blocks of this supply stream—the acquisition process and delivery to the user, with limited involvement in development and involvement with payment only when problems arise.

Supply management, by contrast, serves to manage all facets of the supply stream, including optimizing the actual use. This entire supply chain is the new domain of the sup-

Figure 3-2. The complete supply stream.

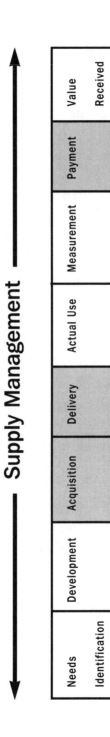

ply manager and a platform for optimizing total costs and performance.

By the early 1990s, a few procurement leaders had begun performing major surgery on their procurement processes. In doing so, they created an opportunity to begin a new process by asking, "What are we trying to do here? How can we be sure we are dealing with the right suppliers, and how can we maximize the value from our purchase expenditures?" These questions led to a variety of "strategic" sourcing initiatives.

As a result, many procurement departments are now consolidating their supplier base and implementing national supplier agreements, as well as introducing new reengineering initiatives. Yet they are still failing to create the strategies necessary to maximize value and minimize their total cost of ownership (the sum of all costs associated with every facet of the supply stream, discussed in more detail in Chapter 4).

As important as supplier base consolidation and procurement reengineering are, when taken alone they leave large gaps in the benefits that can and must be derived for businesses to be viable in today's environment. Supplier consolidation is used largely to facilitate price leverage, and reengineering efforts are generally moves toward simplified release mechanisms for suppliers, such as EDI releases and use of procurement cards. These are usually focused on the beginning part of the supply stream—the needs identification to delivery phases (see Figure 3-2), including the pricing and order issuance steps.

Any number of examples could illustrate some of the gaps in these incomplete processes, but the real-life situation that follows illustrates nearly all in one telling.

Titanium Dioxide Case Study

In 1992, a leading producer of fine paper products was reexamining its roster of suppliers and the value being received for its major purchases. Titanium dioxide was an important ingredient in the company's paper-making process and critical to creating the whiteness and brightness necessary to meet its printer customers' specifications. This manufacturer was a leader with a large share of the market. Not surprisingly, it purchased a lot of titanium dioxide, well over 30 million pounds each year.

Titanium dioxide exists in two chemical forms:

1. *Anatase titanium dioxide*—used by virtually all paper manufacturers to add whiteness to paper
2. *Rutile titanium dioxide*—having a mirror image molecular structure; it is less expensive but not as effective in meeting whiteness specifications and somewhat harder to process

The manufacturer was purchasing approximately 80 to 90 percent of its annual requirements from one U.S. supplier, which had provided its anatase titanium dioxide for a number of years.

The paper producer began its reevaluation process by meeting with the supplier to make sure that it was receiving the lowest possible price per pound. The supplier relationship was supported with a buying contract that included a "most favored customer" clause, ensuring that the paper producer would always receive the best pricing offered to any other customer. They were assured that their $.87-per-pound price was the best. . . . After all, they were a large, valued customer.

The supply leader responsible for titanium dioxide formed a team including technical and operating representatives. Together, they decided to begin some market studies to learn about other suppliers, changes in technology, and changes in processing techniques and also to better understand what pricing other paper producers obtained for titanium dioxide.

Several facts came to light about the same time.

■ At least two other major paper producers were reportedly paying $.85 per pound for the same chemical. One of these producers was also a customer of the same supplier. This price difference would have given this competitor a $1.5–2 million profit advantage at comparable volumes.

■ The paper producer learned that its annual purchase volume of more than 30 million pounds qualified it as the world's single largest purchaser.

■ There were at least five other leading suppliers who were willing to supply titanium dioxide—with the same chemical structure and at the same specifications—for $.81 per pound. (This price reduction alone would create a manufacturing savings of almost $6 million per year.)

Needless to say, these new facts hit the proverbial fan and all previous bets were now off. The paper producer also received a crash course in understanding how little value it was receiving from its current supplier, albeit "protected" by its most favored customer clause and contract.

No matter how the current supplier scurried to make up the pricing difference created by this customer's "shopping" its annual volume needs, the trust was broken and a full-scale market search initiated. This was clearly an example of having over-consolidated suppliers, and failing to protect market leverage.

In the meantime, the paper producer did shift its volume from the one supplier to three new suppliers and received $.81-per-pound pricing from all. With these new cost savings in hand, the supply team began a thorough review of all suppliers worldwide. The review focused on technology and costs and sought the best new long-term partners, those offering the most competitive advantage.

The supply team had not undertaken a comprehensive review of this type in over ten years, so team members were quite surprised to encounter a supplier that claimed to have developed a new manufacturing process for the mirror image version of anatase titanium dioxide—rutile titanium dioxide. The benefits of this new product promised comparable effectiveness in whitening, no process problems, plus offered the added benefit of using 15 percent less in volume. At comparable pricing, this type of volume reduction would provide additional cost savings of $5–6 million per year.

But what new supplier could really pull this off? . . . Du Pont, a supplier that traditionally invests in R&D with the objective of creating tangible, proprietary benefits in functionality or cost. And unlike its smaller competitors, Du Pont has the resources to support a customer that is learning and using its products. In this way Du Pont was able to convince the paper producer to conduct a "trial" of the new material on one of its machines. If the trial went well, the companies were to discuss further expansion to all production locations.

Du Pont is typical of highly successful competitors that leave little to chance. It provided all the technical and logistics resources to stage the line trial:

- It arranged for delivery at $.81 per pound.
- It developed the measuring techniques for on-line usage.
- It suggested that payment be made only for the amount used, thus eliminating inventory costs.
- It monitored usage and delivery.
- It reported volumes requiring payment, eliminating purchase orders, releases, and individual checks, and

switched to electronic funds transfer as the new payment method.

- It provided technical and operating resources to effect
new usage procedures and to familiarize operators
with the new material.

At the end of the trial, the 15 percent usage reduction
target was well exceeded.

What began as a simple "value check" resulted in understanding that this raw material was sourced from a world-
wide market of capable suppliers, all clamoring to reward
large customers.

Immediate price benefits for consolidating with the right
suppliers were supplemented by longer-term, greater benefits
in technology and costs.

In addition to significantly altering its cost position, the
paper producer benefited from the changes made to the delivery stream itself. Gone were the schedulers of railcars, the
internal production planners forecasting volume, the countless paper releases for each production shift, and the invoices
and receipts. The focus shifted to effectiveness at point of
use and how to utilize the capable supplier resources to continue to create improvements at point of use.

This new focus is what supply management is all
about.

IMPLEMENTATION GUIDE

1. In discussions with your organization's procurement
professionals, initially question whether they are consolidating the supply base.

- Ask if they know the reason (it should go well beyond price).
- Do they know all the relevant elements of total cost?
- Do they plan continuous year-over-year budgeted improvements?
- Do you understand these so that you can be effective in eliminating any barriers to your staff's progress?

2. Ask about cycle time—from design to manufacturing, from definition of need to actual fulfillment, from purchase order to payables, and so on—whatever is important to your customers or is of benefit to your business.

- Do they know these times?
- Do they understand how they're important?
- Are there measurements in place?

3. Ask about the actual buying processes.

- Have these processes been redesigned to eliminate non-value-adding steps?
- Are they simple?
- Are they consistent?
- Are they effective?

4. Ask about how the acquired goods or services are actually used.

- Is there a process map?
- Does your team understand customer requirements, internal and external?

5. Ask about product quality and consistency.

- Are these measured? Chances are production materials are well measured by process capability, parts per million, defect rate, or some other defined method. But it's just as important to measure less-tangible elements in indirect material or service areas.
- Can the impact of quality variables be described? Subjective is okay. Just do it.

6. Ask about procurement strategies.

- Are there any strategies beyond price?
- Is the total cost concept understood?
- Is the organization linked to business objectives, customer needs?

7. All of these questions are addressed as we further develop the supply management concept, but the above questions are a great start. "No" responses are where you come in.

- Are these questions important?
- Is there a roadblock you should be helping to eliminate? Is there need for better communication across the organization?

CHAPTER 4

The Marketplace
Twenty-First Century—
Change and Time

When interest in procurement savings increased in the late 1980s, the motivation was simple profit improvement to hedge a tough economy, corporate restructures, and the competitive pressure of global markets. As a result, most companies we know now claim to be focused on some program to improve procurement performance.

Yet, as significant as these pressures are, major corporations are achieving only partial success in any form of procurement implementation. Why? Are the rewards not large enough? Do they lack skills and leadership? Is the solution too complicated? If the business and market environment were to remain the same as it is today, we could probably continue to debate this issue (if we could summon the interest) for another ten years and only marginally improve the implementation success rate.

As luck would have it, markets never stay the same. The marketplace, for all businesses, changes every day. In fact, the pervasive infusion of information technology into every facet of business is creating not just new opportunities for change, but a growing demand for drastically new processes to meet these changing business and market needs. As we prepare for this impact in the next century, we will be behind before we begin if we accept new process solutions that require longer than one year to implement.

We say this with absolute certainty, simply because the new paradigm for success is *time*—time, and how to use time to secure competitive advantage.

If time is so important, why are so many companies taking forever to implement any form of procurement improvement, beginning with simple supplier consolidation? Could it be they are missing the link between suppliers and their time-to-market?

The twenty-first-century marketplace is changing the rules and means to success. Without competence in the supply side of its business, a company will not be able to compete.

Time Is Competitive Advantage

For years, Tom Peters has been providing insights to successful businesses based on the benefits of obsessive focus and "just do it" cultural styles. The underpinning of this success all along has been a business's ability to capitalize on *time*—the improved time-to-market with new products, new features, new services, new uses.

The benefits of a time advantage are being widely documented by business academics and major consulting firms. A number of studies have concluded that it is better to be as much as 50 percent over budget but on time than to be on budget and six months late, because you can never recover the lost market rewards over the life of the project.

One marketing leader at a major telecommunications company described the impact of deregulation as "impending doom." His main concern was his organization's inability to shorten its *time-to-market* for new services in order to compete with new market entrants. "Currently we require thirty-six months to develop new products," he told us. "Even if we shorten that to twenty-four months, we can't compete with new companies that can make changes in six months."

This lack of mobility is fairly typical of large organized development programs. All the experimentation with other models for quick implementation—skunkworks, "intrapreneurial" programs, venture groups, and live prototyping—is targeted at creating new processes to shorten time. Yet, here we sit with this bureaucratic procurement process that takes three pieces of paper for each purchase order, three approvals, fifty-two handoffs from procurement to suppliers to internal users, and a cycle time of at least one year to incorporate new changes that are supporting these development processes. Even if a few spirited venture types can bootleg a purchase directly with a supplier, some poor slug ultimately has to backtrack, fill in the paperwork, and try to get the supplier paid.

We keep missing the point! This isn't about buying "stuff" or checking to make sure we paid the right amount. This is about how suppliers can get us to the market faster and how we can be better when we get there.

When is the last time you met with key suppliers for your business to discuss this kind of opportunity? Never? We're not surprised. No one considers the supply stream as a vital process link for cycle time any more than for improved profitability.

If we are all sniffing around the edges of valuing time as a dimension of success, the sheer acceleration of applied information technology will create a demand for new time standards by the year 2000. Thankfully this may force us to blow up our procurement processes as they exist today in order to survive. Importantly for you, the executive leader is uniquely positioned to create new principles and values based on time as a measure and the role of cycle time as a dimension of process effectiveness.

Marketing consulting firms, such as Boston Consulting Group, have numerous case studies of global market supremacy based on seizing cycle time advantages to market.

Roger Milliken of Milliken Textiles redefined his company's leadership position in a sagging textile industry suffering the invasion of offshore labor through redefining the time-to-market for his customer's customer. Simply, he shortened the development cycle, originally at thirty-six months, to six months from fiber to clothing at the retail shelf. In this case, it was Milliken the supplier who provided the leadership and catalyst for change. For Milliken and his customers, time became competitive advantage.

Suppliers and new supply processes can dramatically alter a company's cycle time for improvements and new products. In fact, the supplier bears the responsibility for managing these supplies and services as you would manage one of your own supporting technologies.

Chrysler has demonstrated this effectively in the auto industry with substantially improved development cycles for new cars. Chrysler, not as vertically integrated as GM, relies heavily on suppliers to collaborate in the development cycle, including implementation of improvements as they are developed. This has shortened Chrysler's development cycle to thirty-three months as compared to General Motors' forty-six months. Even GM's current engineering process redesign is only targeting a new cycle time of thirty-eight months, still five months behind Chrysler.

Thomas Stallkamp, business leader for large auto projects at Chrysler, talked to *Forbes* magazine in 1996 about suppliers' input into the engineering process. "We don't have any seat engineers anymore," he said. "They're managing the programs with seat suppliers instead of developing seats."

Chrysler's new design center actually colocates its engineers and designers with suppliers' resources to encourage the ultimate in collaboration and shorter cycle time. These examples are all emerging as part of a new way to harness supply-side potentials.

Virtual Corporations Depend Heavily on New Supply Strategies

As corporations prepare for the next century marketplace, they have begun to focus on those core competencies that will distinguish their products or services in that marketplace. The restructuring of businesses is already underway, aimed at increasing business focus and capability in its core skills.

A virtual corporation is a business that retains in its direct control only those assets and skills directly related to the specific competence it uses to create its product or service. This could consist of a single skill—design, logistics, or customer service—or a portion of added-value manufacturing. In any example, this business relies on the marketplace to provide its "supporting technologies." Supporting technologies is another way to think about all the materials and services needed to run a business. These include component parts, raw materials, supplies, office support, services, temporary labor, and benefits—all of which, while not vital to the virtual corporation's product or competence, are necessary to support the success of the business entity. In this way, the virtual corporation relies upon the suppliers to manage these "technologies" as though they were actually a part of the business structure. This is outsourcing at its finest, requiring the very best supplier leadership to manage these suppliers as though they were part of the business R&D staff.

Clearly, new supply strategies must be created to meet the demand of these new types of businesses. They must encompass the total supply stream, continuously improve cost and value, and be ever mindful of implementing best practices, new features, and, ultimately, innovations. The procurement process was never like this. And that's the point: The competitive marketplace will both demand and create supply-side strategies to support our businesses, and allow us to focus our employees on the essence of what it is we do.

A new method of engaging this marketplace and creating and managing these strategies, however, must replace the antiquated procedural supplier processes of the past.

Every company is seeking to become some form of "virtual corporation." All differ in dimension and complexity, but it's only a matter of time before they choose to rely on the marketplace for managing their "supporting technologies." The only thing missing is what process they will use.

Supply Networks to Create Market Influence

Some organizations have begun to form collaborative networks that help them to enter markets, and use their combined leverage to influence cost, access to technology, and speed.

An air-travel consortium has been formed with the mission of reengineering the business travel purchase process, to provide group purchasing opportunities, to share expertise among participants, and to administer agreements. The aim is to shift agency fees from commissions to fees for service, and to shift airline charges to airfares, away from commissions and overrides. The intent is to simplify and take the cost out of the administrative process by allowing a clear connection between the sellers (airlines) and the buyers (companies) rather than the confusing, cross-purpose identification of individuals and agencies as customers.

Consortium buying in several forms has become an important strategy for at least four of the Regional Bell Operating Companies ("Baby Bells") who purchase cellular telephones, personal communications devices, infrastructure equipment, and computer hardware and software in this manner. According to *NAPM Insights* (August 1995), ". . . organizations continue to explore consortium partnerships, which tout cost savings, improved quality, and joint learning of professional techniques and strategies."

The consortium idea is here to stay, and provides a means of combining the strengths of independence and flexibility with the power of the group. Some are administered by for-profit companies; other are self-administered.

From a slightly different perspective, many companies have encouraged a collaboration of their suppliers to more effectively devise solutions to their product development equation. These frequently yield superior technology and a time-to-market advantage in key areas or assemblies that otherwise would not have been possible.

This tightening of the supply chain provides genuine competitive advantage.

Honda, for example, and other progressive assembly businesses frequently have several suppliers working together on various subassemblies. One supplier may or may not be identified as the assembler, but they leverage their collective expertise and actually co-develop the assembly.

Access to Supply Markets for Best Practices

The multitudes of traditional buyers have been accessing markets for years in search of suppliers and prices. A by-product of this search is a wealth of knowledge about the suppliers' practices and processes, all of which contributes to their product quality, costs, and pricing. This knowledge however, rarely gets shared with the ultimate user of the product. As a result, the user is denied the opportunity to improve his or her usage patterns, techniques, processes, and ultimate effectivenesses. *This is part of the new learning. The most competitively advantaged businesses bring with them a wealth of practice and process expertise that can be used to re-design the purchaser's usage process.* Clearly, Chrysler has figured this out, which is why the co-location and co-development of designs are integral to their new product success.

The new world of supply management unleashes the traditional buyer from his or her bonds of paper and procedures, and frees the buyer to search the market for the best ways to manage the "supporting technologies" he or she buys. As you can imagine, this buyer begins asking a whole array of different questions on a variety of issues. (Figure 4-1).

Figure 4-1. Market exploration issues.

Traditional Buyers	Supply Managers
■ Ability to meet specifications ■ Price ■ Contract terms ■ Delivery	■ Search for most competitively advantaged supplier ■ Technology analysis ■ Understanding best usage practices ■ Supplier cost analysis ■ Search for best customer experiences and learning ■ Manage the supplier relationship

The supply manager has relinquished the "don't ask questions—just get it here" mentality for a new approach that quickly builds his or her skill as a market and/or technology expert. This type of buyer cannot only describe which technology to use, but what it should cost, how best to use it, store it, evaluate it, improve it, and, finally, which supplier is best equipped with resources to help you implement its use. This buyer has benchmarked with other customers who may have already implemented portions of best practices and have hard data targets as guidelines for success. This buyer will deliver the best product at the best cost with the best process for use, all culminating in supply strategy that optimizes the total cost of ownership. The buyer has selected a supplier with a leading competitive advantage. And there is a high likelihood that the supplier will retain his or her leadership position for a number of years.

We have seen this enlightened approach successfully work across a myriad of supply streams and watched buyers who have accrued the skills to become market and process experts. Their new abilities become your business's point of access to these supply markets. They, in essence, become the portal to the purchased supporting technologies. But their mission is clearly different from that of the traditional buyer.

Now, this buyer-role transformation is exciting and all well and good. However, the big payoff derives from the immediacy of results the buyers deliver. These buyers are best positioned to utilize your company leverage with the most competitively advantaged suppliers.

As a result, at the point of purchase, you will have received the best match of product/service, quality, and price. This rematching alone will almost always generate cash savings. The larger payoff comes from introducing these products or services into your business with "best-usage practices." This strategy for use will optimize usage effectiveness, eliminate waste and inventories, improve output, reduce employee time, etc. The benefits are accrued at point of use. Said another way: The benefits are immediate.

This ability to generate immediate results is what fuels our excitement about blowing up the old process and entering the new world. Simply, if you can prepare to access the supply markets in a new way, you can tap real cash potentials and deliver short-term results. When was the last time anyone promised your business a big fix in the short term? The key, of course, is to capture this potential for virtually every supply stream. This will require a radical departure from old procedures and several gallons of leadership to fuel the way.

Supply Strategies Become the New Platform for Technology and Skill

Clearly, this isn't as easy as an unstructured romp through the marketplace, and voila!—short-term profit improvement! Each purchased supply or service will require a definitive strategy for its purchase and use. The good news is that the supplier, if chosen correctly, can help to create and implement this strategy. This simple platform is the key to securing the best technology and skill for the utilization of this supporting technology. So, whether we are purchasing plastic components, corporate travel, or small hand-tools, we want to be certain we have selected the best technology with the best-usage practices, the best access, and the best delivery processes at the best costs. The only way we know to do that is to *create a strategy that specifies those simple dimensions.*

Figure 4-2 shows a simplistic but typical supply strategy that might be developed by the automotive consumable supply manager, responsible for purchasing tires for a garden tractor company. He and his team of operatives studied the marketplace and their own tire usage, and developed a plan to consolidate their tire purchases with two suppliers. The suppliers, in turn, helped the supply team to standardize twenty-two different tire specifications into four standard products, varying only by size. The inventory savings alone offset the increased costs for standardizing to higher quality levels for all tires. This program was implemented in 1996. The supply leader and team have gone on to implement other improvements in the total supply process.

These included:

- *Delivery to point of use:* eliminating all on-site inventories. Suppliers deliver tires twice per operating shift to points of installation.
- *Ordering and paying process:* eliminating the internal

Figure 4-2. Typical supply stream.

Garden Mower/Tractor Tires—1998

Purchased material or service supplier(s)	Mower/tractor tires from Goodyear, Michelin, Toyo
Standard product or tailor-made—quality specifications specified	4 standard tires 6", 8", 10", 11"
Volume & use characteristics	300,000 per size/year 1,000/size per 3-shift day
Delivery to point of use	Supplier delivers real time to production line staging 6 times/day Annual pricing contract wire transfer funds/daily based on # of tires consumed
Best-usage practices	Pay for use, no inventory, no scrap/waste, paperless process
Key improvements to current process	■ Tire life development ■ New installation kit ■ Employee training
Benchmarking for success	Ford, Saturn ■ Effectiveness in use 1,000 of 1,002 tires ■ Maintenance cost $136/25 cars
Key measures for success	■ Availability/quality ■ Utilization effectiveness ■ Installation time ■ Cycle time for improvements ■ Quality performance review
Resources & accountability	■ Supply leader: J. Smith ■ Goodyear maintenance engineer

	■ Michelin trainers
Financial impact	■ $ savings
	■ Cycle time changes
	■ Customer satisfaction

scheduling and purchase order/release against contract/invoicing process. Replace with pay on consumption policy and nightly electronic funds transfer. Each tractor that is officially counted to meet quality finished production is used to measure actual tire usage. Suppliers are paid based on actual *use*. A general performance contract is in place; pricing adjustments are negotiated annually.

This strategy reflects these process improvements and usage practices as well as planned improvements for 1997. Planned improvements include:

- *Tire life development.* Product improvement to extend tire life by three months.
- *New installation kit.* Pre-staged installation kit development to shorten installation time by 30 percent.
- *Employee training.* Quality/defect training to improve utilization rate.

The strategy also reflects annual benchmarking studies of utilization rates and maintenance costs at automobile manufacturers known for leading-edge practices.

Finally, the strategy defines key performance measures, periodic review schedules, and defined leadership and resources accountability. The output is defined in specific dollar savings, cycle time, and customer satisfaction measures.

For some time, procurement leaders have been developing strategies similar to this for critical manufacturing materials. However, they take any number of forms—some so complicated and filled with specifics that the participants get lost in the organic detail. The missing opportunity is to create this level of careful planning and optimization for *all major supply streams.* For example, a $5.0MM transportation purchase is just as deserving as a $5.0MM garden tractor tire purchase of a strategy to optimize its use and total cost. These strategies can be just as powerful for corporate travel, health-care benefits, maintenance services, and a whole platform of nontraditional purchasing areas. In fact, the short-term values may be even greater because these areas have never received this level of scrutiny or optimization. The role of the new supply management process is to provide simple processes and mechanisms to help create and successfully manage these strategies.

The strategy itself is the platform for defining the specific technology, practice, and process improvements necessary to create optimum use and cost. At a glance, the strategy defines the opportunities and skills necessary for success. In essence, the strategy is the perfect leadership language to provide focus for direction, set priorities, measure results, and change direction.

IMPLEMENTATION GUIDE

Your supply management process going into the next century must respond to your market demands for new levels of performance and process cycle time. The following questions provide you a guide to engage your procurement and operating leaders in a process to begin this change.

1. Do specific stream strategies exist in your business?

- For which material and services?
- What form do these take?
- Who develops and implements these?
- Who reviews results and earnings?

2. What regular benchmarking processes do you use to scan the market for best practices and processes?

- Is this done regularly for major supply streams?
- For all supply streams?

3. What organizational groups meet to review best-usage practices and procedures?

- Best-usage performances among your locations?

4. Have you or anyone defined specific measures for success for each supply stream?

5. Do you know the actual cycle time for your product/ service development?

- Time from sourced components through product design, manufacture, and delivery?

6. Have you reviewed the process alternatives for shortening development or manufacturing cycles?

- What are these?
- How do they work?
- Who are companies with the most success?

7. Do your supply managers know the cycle time for each purchase stream?

■ How much is waiting time vs. working time?

The supply management process and its mechanisms are designed to fill in these blanks and provide a simple structure to create supply strategies for all supply streams.

The following chapters offer descriptions of how to manage these purchase expenditures while capturing the potential of the marketplace as it develops.

CHAPTER 5

Supply Management: Strategy and Process

In today's competitive marketplace, where every business is striving to reduce its cost of delivering more distinctive products or services to customers, businesses can no longer ignore the importance of purchased materials and services by treating them as non-value-adding transactions.

The competitive marketplace demands a new management process using focused concepts and tools to reevaluate business purchasing behavior. Supply management, a new source of competitive advantage, is just that process. This chapter describes the key concepts and benefits of the supply management process and tells you how to realize and measure those benefits. With this process you can improve your costs, increase your quality consistently, generate improvements for your customers, and shorten the cycle time for bringing these improvements to the marketplace.

A New Source of Competitive Advantage

Definition: *supply management:*

1. A methodology to examine all facets of the buying and actual use of purchased materials and services.

2. A new business process designed to maximize the value of dollars spent on purchased materials and services.

Supply management differs from traditional procurement processes in two major ways:

1. *It is not just about buying stuff.* It is a process that creates strategies to manage the overall procurement and use of materials or services.
2. *It is an "outside-in process."* It is a process that enables the buyer to proactively determine the values that best serve its needs in the marketplace, a radically different approach from issuing bidding requests and reacting to marketplace response.

As shown in Figure 5-1, the supply management process focuses on optimizing the entire delivery stream: all the steps from the identified need through the delivery of the sourced material/service; its use, measurement, and payment; and the value created for the end customer.

The new role of the supply manager is to access the marketplace through a network of the "best suppliers," which provide:

- Best fit to meet required needs and benefits
- Best technology
- Best practices
- Best processes
- Best cost structures
- Best time to market

The supply manager and the supplier create a strategy to implement an improved "delivery system" that includes

Figure 5-1. The material service stream.

best practices for actual usage, measurement, and all supporting processes and transactions.

We refer to supply management as a new source for competitive advantage because its benefits are both sizable and far-reaching. It is the one single business process you can use to directly link key suppliers to key customers. In this way you can explore myriad new market possibilities as part of your short-range plans. For example, by linking component manufacturers into the company's development and engineering cycle, multiple new technologies can be evaluated and combined to achieve a record time-to-market and new levels of creativity.

Supply management is a perfect complement for decentralized business structures because it provides all the benefits of total business leverage (heretofore achieved only through large, centralized structures) with all the advantages of localized implementation. This is possible by using standardized processes. It builds on the knowledge that process standardization is replacing the organizational structures and systems that guided businesses in the past, thus allowing for consistent, reproducible results. In so doing, it is allowing businesses to redefine their work tasks, to eliminate all but those that directly add value to the customer.

What Is It?

The supply management process is a leading-edge strategic management process that:

- Manages all purchased materials and services to reduce costs.

- Focuses suppliers on improvements in quality, consistency, and usage.
- Harnesses a supplier's resources to create new product or service features for a business's customers with faster cycle time to market (the suppliers are the experts in their fields).

It is an all-encompassing business strategy with four key requirements:

1. A cross-company process, as opposed to a nonfunctional or departmental approach
2. Companywide use of integrated supply processes with best-in-class suppliers
3. Alliances among internal and external resources, including people, assets, and technologies, focused on continual improvement and innovation for competitive advantage
4. Management training and education in world-class supply management techniques: internal and external market analysis, strategic cost understanding, and process reengineering

Supply management organizes work according to the actual flow of a purchased material or service to the end customer, as shown in Figure 5-2. The main purpose is to optimize the ultimate value to your customer.

The supply management process is designed to provide specific utility and functionality for each supply stream by:

- Identifying the best suppliers.
- Analyzing all related industry and cost/usage practices.

Figure 5-2. Material/service work flow.

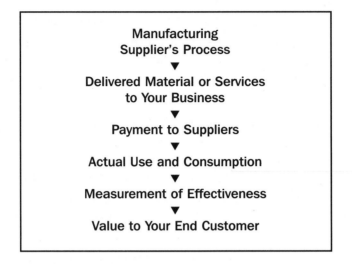

Manufacturing
Supplier's Process
▼
Delivered Material or Services
to Your Business
▼
Payment to Suppliers
▼
Actual Use and Consumption
▼
Measurement of Effectiveness
▼
Value to Your End Customer

- Revealing the cost of purchase, receipt, inventory, and payment.
- Determining the actual employee use and time impacts.
- Relating material or service value to the end customer's needs and usage.

Supply streams may be single products or services, similar groups of products or services, or sometimes even miscellaneous, dissimilar products or services, grouped for administrative efficiency. Examples include office products, part or all of maintenance support purchases, health care, advertising, tires, fasteners, major production materials or assemblies, and so on.

The effectiveness of the supply process is measured over several dimensions, not just unit cost or acquisition cost:

- Total cash costs, including unit costs, inventory costs, discounts, and interest charges
- Usage costs, including the actual utility value versus best practices, waste, and quality standards
- Process costs, including scheduling, inventory, ordering, receiving, payment, and measurements
- Cycle time from supplier to the end customer

Businesses use the supply management process to focus supplier resources on seeking out and adding best industry practices in all dimensions of the material/service stream. The process can be considered optimized when the time-to-market cycle has become faster than that of competitors.

How Does It Work?

The supply management process enables the supply manager of a particular supply stream to continually improve his or her knowledge of the marketplace, suppliers' costs, and best industry practices. Knowledge of the marketplace and access to it become the platform for continual improvement and the basis for ongoing supply-stream strategies.

The supply management process utilizes three standardized, interrelated processes, shown in Table 5-1, to deliver its benefits. These standardized processes are work steps and approaches that are applied to every supply stream. These three processes—the procurement process, the continual improvement process, and the innovation process—become the centerpiece of a sourcing program that replaces the traditional centralized procurement structure. The processes engage the relevant participants and decision makers in selecting and managing suppliers to

Table 5-1. Supply management core processes.

	Procurement Process	Continual Improvement Process	Innovation Process
	The market and supplier process to determine the best suppliers to meet a material/ service need for cost and quantity	The supplier planning process to guide supplier's resources to material/service optimization and continual improvement in usage and cost	The search to locate and develop leading-edge options for innovation in products and processes
Key Concepts	■ Market/industry analysis ■ Supplier cost models	■ Value chain mapping ■ Total cost of ownership ■ Benchmarking	■ Satisfaction needs analysis ■ Time-based innovation ■ Creating new solutions
Outcomes	■ Best suppliers with most competitive advantage	■ Optimal material/ service cost and use ■ Plan for minimum total cost of ownership	■ Innovation readiness ■ Innovation prototypes
Benefits	■ Supplier consolidation ■ Cost savings	■ Cost savings ■ Employee time savings	■ Revenue improvement ■ Cost improvement

achieve the maximum value for dollars spent. Each of the three processes provides ample freedom to accommodate different needs, different markets, different businesses, different variables.

So whether a supply management leader is responsible for purchasing chemicals or air travel, he or she would utilize these processes to search the market for the best suppliers, engage those suppliers in creating a strategy to optimize materal/service cost and use, and periodically search for innovations in cost or new features that could dramatically change the total cost of ownership (the sum of all costs associated with every facet of the supply stream, discussed in more detail later in this chapter). The supply leader can apply these concepts to address the needs of the total business as well as the needs of different parts of the business. In this way these processes can be used to create global sourcing and managing strategies.

These core processes create outcomes (see Table 5-1) independent of structure, formal job description, functional boundaries, or corporate policy. They are unique, new mechanisms that can help you think differently about each supply you purchase, capitalizing on your size and the best that the market has to offer. Chapter 6 covers in more detail the actual process steps, work tasks, supporting tools, and capabilities.

By applying these processes to each of your supply streams, supply management provides an opportunity to get out a clean sheet of paper and answer these questions: What are we buying? Why? How much do we spend? Who is buying it? From which suppliers?

With those questions in mind, the leadership challenge is to "turn loose" a group of people willing to rethink each supply stream, using these processes as a guide for the questions they need to ask. Not surprisingly, procurement buyers become likely supply leaders *if* they can set aside their old buying practices and gleefully take a new view of the marketplace.

This work is best done in teams, which provide the opportunity to include the internal customers or users in relevant business groups or functional organizations. Payables or systems experts are also included if major surgery on the ordering and paying process is required. (We're assuming your organization has experience working effectively with cross-functional teams. If not, there is a large variety of "how to" literature available on the subject.)

The executive role is to give these teams the freedom necessary to create change, revise policies, standardize products, encourage new procedures where necessary, and, most important, to recognize their results.

These early teams will create models of success. They will change things, they will run into barriers, and they will need help. They will invade people's comfort zones. The next battery of teams will learn from these efforts. They will engage the relevant people up front in the market analysis phase and the decision process. They too will see significant success in such areas as savings, features, service, and better process effectiveness.

It is our experience that implementing the supply management process across thirty supply streams creates a critical mass of involvement, awareness, and credibility to support a complete new supply management review of all purchased materials and services. We personally have implemented the procurement and continual improvement processes in multibillion-dollar corporations in one to two years. Some organizations combine the procurement and continual improvement processes to shorten this implementation time, thereby increasing the magnitude of results.

The key to supply management is to *start* with the expectation that each supply stream can be completely reviewed, the supply base consolidated, and new supply strategies defined within three to six months. If it takes longer than this, the supply team has lost its way and needs help.

Supply Management Concepts

Three platform concepts drive the effectiveness of the supply management work:

1. Market/industry analysis as a lens for supplier selection
2. Value chain mapping as the key to optimizing supply-stream effectiveness, with critical standards of measure, including cycle time to use, cycle time to market, and total cost
3. Total cost of ownership as the new comprehensive measure of effectiveness for the supply-stream strategy

Market/Industry Analysis

Market/industry analysis is an externally oriented activity for selecting a supplier or group of suppliers. This process searches the marketplace characteristics to identify suppliers who can satisfy your needs in a competitively advantaged manner. The suppliers with the most competitive advantage tend to have the following characteristics:

- *They are low-cost producers* who have implemented the most advanced manufacturing technologies or best-practice service concepts to obtain the lowest variable costs.
- *They have the best cost control* with quality processes and supporting systems in delivering consistent results.
- *They have the best new technology and innovation cycles,* with supporting networks of suppliers who bring them leading-edge practices.

- *They are generally first to the marketplace with new improvements* as they claim a leadership position for distinctive products and services.

Market analysis permits the supply manager to study market cycles and business cycles as a way to select suppliers and design a purchasing strategy. Such analysis can help you select the suppliers who can best meet your needs from a cost and technology standpoint and might mean the difference between choosing leading-edge versus trailing-edge technology.

Market analysis results in an entirely different approach to procurement from that of the past. Historically, purchases were made to meet an "internally" defined set of needs. The "specification" grew out of an engineering discipline that presumed the customer's needs would stay the same long enough to build the product and deliver it. Today's marketplace, with its demands for fast change, forces the supply manager to link the buying process to the end customer's needs. This takes the purchaser on a different journey from one to "fill specifications" with the lowest unit cost.

Ongoing market analysis is the cornerstone of the supply management process. It works by examining the market for a particular good or service from a number of perspectives in order to understand its trends, competitive framework, substitutes, cost levers, and strategies for success. With this learning in hand, a supply manager is prepared to begin the search for the "best of the best" suppliers to meet the identified needs.

The market analysis tool we most recommend is the Industry Analysis Model, created by Dr. Michael Porter at Harvard University. Porter's model has been a mainstay of business and marketing strategy for the past twenty years. It is used directly and indirectly by every marketing organization to analyze markets in developing new product, service, or geographic strategies. The model can also be used to determine the best suppliers. Shown in Figure 5-3, Porter's model is based on a five-force view of the marketplace:

- Rivalry among the existing companies
- Bargaining power of customers/buyers
- Threat of new entrants
- Bargaining power of suppliers
- Threat of substitute products or services

Figure 5-3 illustrates how each force influences industry competition and lists areas the supply manager should consider during market analysis. These five forces are at work whether an industry is domestic or international.

The collective strength of these five competitive forces determines the ability of companies in an industry to earn,

Figure 5-3. The Porter Industry Analysis Model.

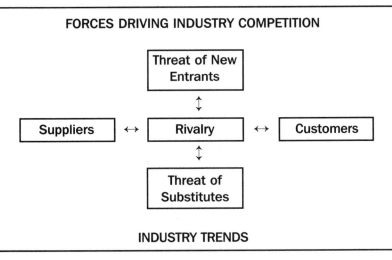

FORCES DRIVING INDUSTRY COMPETITION

INDUSTRY TRENDS

on average, rates of return on investment in excess of the cost of capital. The strength of the forces varies among industries and changes as the industry evolves. Industry profitability is not a function of what the product looks like or whether it embodies high or low technology, but of industry structure.

The five forces determine industry profitability because they influence the prices, costs, and required investment of organizations in an industry—the elements of return on investment. Buyer power and the threat of substitution influence the prices companies can charge. The power of buyers can also influence cost and investment because powerful buyers demand costly service. The bargaining power of suppliers determines the costs of raw materials and other inputs. The intensity of rivalry influences prices as well as the costs of competing in areas such as plant facilities, product development, advertising, and size of sales force. The threat of entry places a limit on prices and shapes the investment required to deter entrants.

Figure 5-4 lists the considerations behind each of these major forces.

Several trends have significant impact on the five competitive forces. For instance, pure competition works toward technical efficiency. If a company is inefficient and producing at a high cost, it will not be able to survive in competition with technically efficient companies that produce at average costs. Intense global competition will quickly drive down costs. Table 5-2 lists some of the trends that affect competition.

The Porter model is also a tremendous platform for understanding strategies, likely changes in the market, new technology directions, and how best to gain market leverage.

Figure 5-4. The Porter Model: considerations.

Threat of New Entrants

Considerations:
- Economies of scale
- Product differentiation
- Capital requirements
- Cost disadvantages independent of size:
  - Learning curve
  - Experience curve
  - Proprietary technology
  - Access to raw materials
- Access to distribution channels
- Government policy; regulated industries or portions of industries

Power of Suppliers	**Industry Competitors—Rivalry**	**Power of Customers/Buyers**
Considerations: ■ Concentration of one type of supplier selling your industry ■ The supplier has the technology that is key to your product ■ Importance of supplied product for your product ■ Availability of substitutes to use in your industry ■ Supplier is likely to integrate forward	*Considerations:* ■ Number of competitors in the industry; size or dominance of industry leaders ■ Product differentiation & switching costs between competitive products ■ Intermittent overcapacity ■ Rate of industry growth—position on life cycle ■ High fixed costs within the industry ■ Rules of the game—difficulty of reading competitive intentions or reactions	*Considerations:* ■ Concentration or large-volume purchases Product purchased is undifferentiated ■ Product purchased is a component that is not significant to the final product's differentiation ■ Product purchased does not save the buyer money ■ Buyer is very price conscious ■ Buyer is likely to integrate backward ■ Retailer/distributor can directly influence end user's buying decision

Threat of Substitution

Considerations:
- Substitutions offer improved price/performance trade-off
- Produced by industries earning higher profits
- Low switching costs to accept substitute
- End user needs and wants

Adapted from Michael E. Porter, *Competitive Advantage* (New York: The Free Press, 1985), p. 6. Reprinted with the permission of The Free Press, a Division of Simon & Schuster. Copyright © 1985.

Table 5-2. Industry trends.

Trend	Examples
Technology	Robotics in manufacturing
Regulatory	Deregulation: airline industry
Global markets	Manufacturing: pricing
Economic	Recession: impact on disposable income
Demographic	Buying power: gray power, baby boomers
Social values	Environment and social issues: plastics, AIDS
Local laws	Same as regulatory, except faster and more focused: smoking

The horizontal forces:

Suppliers	↔	Rivals	↔	Customers

define the economic structure of the industry marketplace.
The vertical forces:

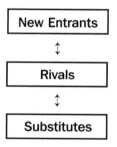

define likely change to an industry marketplace.

Understanding how these forces work and interact is vital in selecting the "best" suppliers for the defined needs of your business.

We recommend that each supply team conduct its market analysis by inviting supplier organizations to present their view of the industry. Remember their market and sales organizations have this information as part of their business planning, so it is an easy way to collect a breadth of information while simultaneously learning how the suppliers think about the market and how they intend to gain or keep their competitive advantage.

At the end of the analysis, the supply team should have a clear view of the following:

- Which supplier has the most competitive advantage
- Which supplier is the low-cost producer/provider
- Which is the distinctive market leader
- What is driving technology change
- Which suppliers control the cost structure

This information allows the team to engage a short list of suppliers for further exploration of their business strategies, costs, and capabilities to help your business optimize its supply stream.

The key question to be asked of every supplier is, "How will we be competitively advantaged if we work with you?" After all, do you want to do business with a supplier who has little or no competitive advantage? (You might be surprised at what lurks in the realm of your master vendor list.) Of course, the only way to be sure is to begin again. It's not a difficult process and it's well worth the effort. Keep in mind that markets change every day. Every day someone merges or fails, new technology creates a shift in cost or benefits, new substitutes replace current products. When we meet supply teams who have been encouraged to take another look at a particular substitute technology and they complain, "We looked at that five years ago!" we know immediately that there is an opportunity to pursue. Businesses that don't improve die, so every year markets offer better and different benefits.

The supply leader must use this market analysis concept

to track industry change and build strategies to capitalize on the opportunities created by it. Market analysis is the single most powerful tool in the supply leader's portfolio of skills. It becomes the compass to help navigate a continually changing business jungle.

Bidding processes and requests-for-information letters somehow fall pitifully short when used as replacements for this type of analysis in selecting suppliers. Supply teams learn how to use this concept by actual application. A typical analysis takes two to four weeks, longer if the industry is composed of many product groupings. By the time a team has applied this concept two or three times, members have developed a solid skill level to effectively chart a course for developing a supply-stream strategy.

The following case of Manpower helps show why it's so important to do the benchmarking and market analysis necessary to identify the best suppliers, those with sound financials, a clear view of the future, the resources, and track record to realize a place in that future. These suppliers will not only prove to be the lowest total cost solution, but will bring you competitive advantage in the form of new ways of thinking about things *if* you listen and have created an atmosphere of listening within your company. Don't assume too narrow a scope when discussing your business needs with suppliers. Assume there are no boundaries. Of course, get a proposal for a specific identified need, but always ask for input on a broader scale. After all, you have identified these companies as leaders in their field. Find out why they are leaders. Most likely, it's because they have capabilities that go well beyond just being the low-cost provider.

Very recently we had an opportunity to spend a morning with Mitchell Fromstein, chairman of Manpower International, Inc., the largest temporary services business in the world. Most people think of Manpower as one of the companies that can supply temporary labor or provide replacement clerical skills when an assistant is sick or goes on vacation. The truth is, the company goes well beyond that by providing and managing turnkey administrative support solutions. It also manages a streamlined temporary labor service for businesses, saving them the administrative costs, and offers electronic timekeeping, which eliminates the non-value-adding steps of signing time cards and invoices for each person. The company also provides electronic summary billing, saving accounts payable time. As in the case of Manpower, if you don't pursue the question "How far can we productively take this relationship?" with your suppliers, you have not done sufficient benchmarking and listening and will miss a lot.

Although most businesses think of Manpower when it's time to add needed supplemental workers or to handle the seasonal blitz of résumés from job seekers, not many think of asking it to manage their entire résumé process. One of its large customers did just that, through an open, inquisitive interchange. In this case, Manpower used its administrative know-how to sort and prioritize résumés, leaving the customer to focus on hiring. The result is a cost-effective solution that plays to the core competencies of each company, and it's continually improving. Good customers, *inquisitive* customers, put their problems, their broad problems, on the line. Manpower offers a breadth of capability, and it works to find a match.

Manpower, through a very large database, keeps the résumés of applicants who are not an immediate fit for the client and often places these people in project work with other clients. If the original client develops a future need, Manpower will have the names tagged and refer them to the company. The client wins, the applicants win, and the supplier wins.

Manpower's business is growing in large part because of the breadth and depth of its client involvement. That's listening. That's continual improvement. You find the company hiring all permanent staff up to an agreed-upon (but rising) level for one large client. You find it not just providing supplemental staff for telephone centers, but providing all staff for the centers, including supervisory personnel. The company has the expertise to establish these centers on a turnkey basis, over and over again.

Relationships like this never happen if a supplier is one of many providers dealt with on a transactional basis. They don't happen without a strategy, a comprehensive supply management strategy that deliberately makes it happen.

Value Chain Mapping

Value chain is a term that denotes a process consisting of a number of related steps, with each step adding a certain value to the total outcome (Figure 5-5). The value chain of a business process, for example, often begins with raw materials, to which a business adds its particular technology. This could be process technology, formula or packaging or ease of use, or some way of transforming the raw materials into a new form of benefits. Manufacturing is often the next step after technology, and it is the value-adding step that uses technology to generate units for sale. The units for sale proceed through a logistics step, which makes them available to the customer, either directly or indirectly through distribution channels. Marketing is the next step and adds the value of positioning, advertising, image, all that is necessary to enhance the features and product benefits. Fi-

Figure 5-5. The business value chain.

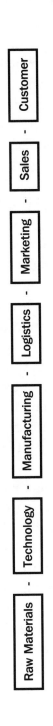

Raw Materials - Technology - Manufacturing - Logistics - Marketing - Sales - Customer

nally, sales adds the final value by meeting customer needs with product sales and service.

Even though tremendously oversimplified, this chain illustrates how each step adds discrete value to the business process output. Maximum process effectiveness, then, is defined as having every task and function in the process as productive as possible. Specific tasks or functions are productive only if they directly add value to the outcome. For example, securing the right raw material with the right qualities and delivering it to the point of use clearly adds value to the business process. However, actually filling out a purchase order, securing approvals, transmitting requisitions to suppliers, and on and on adds no value to the outcome. You may argue that it is necessary until another way can be found to obtain raw material, but it clearly adds no value to the product.

Value chain mapping, then, is the analytical process of examining which steps and tasks add value and which do not. This is the work of creating optimal material and service flow between the source of supply and your customer. Only at this level of inspection and process redesign can you remove all nonessential, non-value-adding work, which, if left in place, adds increased cost and time to meeting the ultimate customer's need.

Value chain mapping is the key to unlocking process gridlock and achieving maximum process effectiveness. To begin, the supply manager and the selected suppliers map the complete steps of providing a material or service, proceeding from the supplier to the end user, including its delivery and use. What emerges is a picture of the intricate interlocking steps that span the supplier and purchaser relationship. The opportunities for change emerge from seeking three goals:

1. Best/lowest total cost, including all process, transactional, and handling costs
2. Best/fastest cycle time, including cycle time to implement improvements
3. Best-usage practices versus best-industry or best-
   technology practices

Changes frequently begin with eliminating redundant
processing and transactional steps in both companies, for
example, eliminating outgoing and incoming quality
checks or matching receiving documents with invoices and
with purchase orders. None of these tasks track the ultimate user's order receipt or satisfaction. Instead, they have
become surrogates that support outdated audit processes.
These changes give the buyer more time to focus on more
fundamental changes, for example, improvements in
equipment handling and implementing best-practice usage
techniques. This becomes the new continual improvement
work of the supply manager.

You can create a value chain map by constructing a detailed representation of all the steps involved in the process
or flow of a product or service from raw material or creation to end-user consumption or use. This part of the tech-
nique is like every other process flowchart you may have
seen. The difference in value chain mapping is that each
step is then categorized into three types of work, as shown
in Figure 5-6:

1. *Value-adding.* Those tasks or work steps directly required to create the product or service.
2. *Essential.* Those tasks or work steps necessary to
   support a function but in and of themselves adding
   no direct value to the finished product or service.
3. *Non-value-adding.* Those tasks or work steps neither

necessary nor required to meet cost or quality standards for a given product or service.

For example, the actual manufacturing process clearly adds value to the inputs to its process. Its outputs meet very definable cost and quality standards that have a value in the marketplace (i.e., customer revenue). The maintenance activities to support this process are necessary to keep the process functioning but do not of themselves add value to the product. The actual steps to provide ordering parts and supplies needed for maintenance are not even essential—if some other

Figure 5-6. Value chain map of a typical purchase process.

Value-Adding Work Steps	Essential Work Steps	Non-Value-Adding Work Steps
		Fill Out Purchase Order
		↓
	Purchase Order to Supplier ←	Approve Purchase Order
	↓	
Supplier Manufactures Product ←	Supplier Schedules Production	
→	Supplier Delivers Product →	Receiving Accepts Product and Calls User
		↓
User Uses Product ←	User Receives Product ←	User Arranges For Delivery

means could be used to ensure their availability, these steps could be eliminated. Simply, they add no value. The clear bias in examining these steps, as with all steps in the entire process, from identifying the need, to the value received by the user, should be, "Don't reengineer it. Eliminate it!"

Michael Hammer, in his book *Reengineering the Corporation*, has documented many case studies of processes filled with non-value-adding tasks and work steps. These tasks and work steps generally are the result of policies and procedures created in history. Over time, they have created the need for forms, approvals, and schedules—"hand-offs" from one function to the next, and on and on—all non-value-adding steps.

Hammer and other experts contend that 90 percent of most business processes are composed of non-value-adding work steps. The value chain mapping process allows you to look across all the steps in your business processes and your supply stream and eliminate as much non-value-adding work as possible. It also allows you and your suppliers to review practices for maximizing the impact of the value-adding steps in your actual use of a product or service. Because you have selected the "best suppliers," those offering the most competitive advantage, they bring best-process and best-practice capability as a part of their product or service offerings. They provide the expert input into the redesign process.

We recommend that each supply team and its preferred supplier(s) complete a value chain mapping analysis. Clearly, this level of analysis cannot be completed with thirty suppliers of a given material or service; it should be developed *after* the supplier consolidation decisions have been made.

At the end of the analysis, the supply team and the supplier develop a list of improvement opportunities, which become the basis of the continual improvement work. These opportunities span every facet of the supply stream, including ordering, delivery, usage, measurement, payment, and supply-stream application and process learning.

Frequently, the easiest improvements are in designing and implementing new ordering, scheduling, and payment steps. This work frees up resource time in your business and the supplier's, allowing you both to focus on enriching the value-added work.

Before actual changes are made to the physical flow of the product or service, the supply team should research other leading-edge customers to seek out best-usage practices. These might include, for example, new inventory tracking methods, application processes for chemicals, programs to help control air travel costs, training curricula, packaging techniques—any practice or method that improves the effectiveness of any facet of the supply stream or of a supply's use. This knowledge of best-usage practices in conjunction with supplier expertise provides the platform for choices necessary to optimize the supply stream. Traditionally, the procurement department of an organization would not dare venture to change the usage patterns of the actual end users of purchased materials and services.

The late W. Edwards Deming, one of the most capable and best-known leaders of the total quality movement, often stated that one of the major problems with procurement people is their lack of understanding of the usage of products in the various stages of manufacturing operations. That is certainly true of manufacturing, and it is equally true of products and services used in service businesses. It isn't enough to simply buy a product or contract for a service and assume that everything will be satisfactory, nor should you assume that the requester knows the optimum use of the product or service. Supply management professionals must be actively engaged in understanding usage. The supply team, therefore, must include representative actual users who can bring internal "user expertise" to help evaluate new options for improvement.

Finally, the supply team (including the suppliers) builds a continual improvement implementation plan complete with tangible outputs and measurements. A detailed list of required resources and responsibilities is formulated at this point and, more often than not, is implemented within your business process by the supplier. This process should take no longer than one or two months and result in an improvement plan ready for implementation.

Total Cost of Ownership

Many types of costs are associated with the supply stream. The total cost of ownership of the supply delivery system is the sum of all costs associated with every facet of the supply stream. Figure 5-7 depicts the types of costs associated with the major steps of the supply stream.

The total cost of ownership (TCO) formula, shown in Figure 5-8, collects these various costs.

The present value concept is used to discount the anticipated future costs over the life cycle of the material or service stream. For example, if a new pump is expected to last ten years, the total costs must be computed for the ten-year cycle and discounted to reflect the current cost.

The simple fact is, no one in the supply chain actually understands the value of all these costs. Furthermore, it would probably take a lifetime to collect the data to measure these costs for just one supply stream. The TCO formula is really a representation of the various aspects of cost and allows the supply team to estimate the cost magnitude, rather than achieve accuracy to the fourth decimal point. It provides the supply team with a way of *scoping* costs in the major supply-stream steps so that the team can identify and place a value on opportunities for improvement.

Figure 5-7. Supply stream costs.

Identified Need	Acquisition	Delivery	Payment	Usage	Measurement	Value to User
Purchase Order Cost	Acquisition Price	Receiving Freight	Payables Process Costs	Training Costs	Laboratory Evaluation	Training Costs
Internal Meeting Time	Inventory Cost	Warehousing On-Hand Inventories	Bank Charges	Quantity/ Use	Quality Control	Communication
	Payment Terms	Storeroom Costs	System Maintenance	Waste Defects	Receiving Process	
	Discount or Rebates	Internal Transpor- tation		Preparation Processes	Usage Measures	
	Purchase Process Costs			Maintenance Repairs		
	Scheduling Process Costs			Recycling Scrap		

Figure 5-8. Total cost of ownership (TCO).

TCO = A + Present Value of (O + T + M + W + E − S)

Total Cost of Ownership

A	=	Acquisition cost
O	=	Operating costs
T	=	Training costs
M	=	Maintenance costs
W	=	Warehousing costs
E	=	Environmental costs
S	=	Salvage value

The most important insight it gives your supply team is the understanding that the acquisition cost itself is often a very small part of the total cost. Typical ratios of acquisition cost to total cost are summarized in Table 5-3.

Focusing on TCO does not diminish the importance of achieving the best acquisition cost possible. Related tools, such as supplier cost analysis and "should cost" modeling, are available to help your supply team determine the optimum cost/price relationship. The TCO analysis does, however, underscore the full magnitude of supply management accountability and the areas for improvement.

The single largest opportunity in developing total cost models is identifying *how* a material or service is best used. This is often a new focus for materials managers because it

Table 5-3. Average acquisition cost as a percentage of total cost of ownership.

Purchased materials	
Manufacturing business	25–35%
Assembly business	50%+
Purchased services	75–90%

takes them into the operating domain of the actual user. But therein is the opportunity to reexamine usage practices and procedures vis-à-vis those of the best practitioners in the marketplace—the actual users. The result is the development of a new usage strategy incorporating the best practices of the most-experienced users. This is the fundamental reason for seeking out "best suppliers"—they are aptly positioned to bring you these usage practices and processes.

Usage measures must be customized by material or service stream and data collected at the point of use. Specific information to be tracked includes how much is consumed, how much is actually utilized, how long it lasts, and how efficiently and effectively it is used. The supply manager must then analyze the data versus industry benchmarks. This is the leading-edge practice for identifying best-usage effectiveness.

The really good professional supply leaders focus on improving usage practices long before conducting total cost modeling. The issue is that, at best, this work is completed before modeling for purchased materials critical to a product's manufacture. Examples are major raw materials, processing equipment, and highly specialized technical skills. The opportunity we describe here stems from applying the total cost model to *all* supply streams in a consistent way.

Implementing the Core Processes

Earlier in this chapter we illustrated the supply management core processes (see Table 5-1). This might just be the most important chart in the book. It certainly is the best crib note on the subject. It's as close as we get to a wallet card primer.

Each of these core processes has distinct benefits and the processes are typically attacked in series, but there is no reason to be limited to that approach. If the team has a clear vision and there are capable and willing suppliers to call upon, engage the processes in parallel. The case study that follows shows how one company did it.

Mellon Bank, N.A., a large and well-run financial services company and the parent of the Dreyfus Corporation, was able to simultaneously implement the procurement process and the continual improvement process in many instances as it moved through the early stages of its supply management journey.

Paper forms represent a multimillion-dollar expenditure for the company. It quickly consolidated its supplier base, reducing the number of suppliers from five to one using a standard sourcing process as shown in Table 5-4. The instant result was a ten percent drop in acquisition cost. At the same time, the acquisition process (see Figure 5-6) was value chain mapped, resulting in faster response time and lower costs with an overall simpler process. A Mellon warehouse was closed, eliminating duplicate inventories. A supplier team was located on-site, eliminating a hand-off step and putting the supplier in closer touch with the end user. A continual improvement goal with firm measurements was established not only to take inflation out of the equation but to ensure year-after-year real cost reduction. Service levels and quality levels were both tracked, with tenfold improvements in each at the end of the first year. The company was able to implement standardization for the first time simply because it was dealing with a single supplier. Forms became more standardized because of a single producer. Use of corporate logos and

Table 5-4. Standardized sourcing process.

■ Establish team	■ Select bidders
■ Define and analyze needs	■ Develop evaluation
■ Market analysis	criteria
Goods and services	■ Develop and issue an RFP
Industry	(request for proposal)
Supply base	■ Select top contenders
■ Benchmarking/best	■ Set targets
practices	■ Determine best suppliers
■ Solidify work scope	■ Make final selection and
■ Select potential bidders	award
Request for	■ Sign contract
bidder conference	■ Implement new supplier
■ Adjust work scope if	access and usage
required	procedures
	■ Measure pricing and
	usage vs. prior period
	■ Establish continual
	communications loop

other printed forms was easily monitored—by the supplier. Measurements were established for all critical indicators. The entire relationship shifted to focus on innovative uses of forms.

By the end of the first year, total costs were down by just under 20 percent for those supply streams implemented. The Procurement and Continual Improvement Processes were implemented concurrently, with benefits from each beginning at the onset. The Innovation Process was producing results by the third year—all as a direct result of the supply management process.

As improvement reviews occurred, questions arose such as, "What are we trying to accomplish here? Why do we need a form?" Voila! Innovation! Electronic solutions were found, and process changes were implemented. Soon, forms became indicators of business processes that needed improvement and often led to completely overhauling entire business processes.

In another supply area, furniture purchases were consolidated with the premier manufacturer. Acquisition processes were mapped and streamlined, standardization was automatically accomplished, and greater volume allowed acquisition cost reduction. The more interesting aspect was the closer, better-integrated relationship between Mellon management and the supplier in optimizing resource capability, providing a natural solution to a difficult and expensive problem. Custom-built furniture and surroundings had been planned for new retail financial centers but were turning out to be expensive and not very durable. Some "outside the box" collaboration with the furniture provider yielded a new product variation that not only solved the Mellon problem but became a standard for the provider. Lower cost. Ready availability. Increased durability. Solutions such as this simply do not happen without consolidation and the continual improvement and innovation expectations set out in supply management guidelines.

In both of these examples, total costs dropped and the expectation of improvement led to breakthroughs. In both, Mellon began by the book by benchmarking best-practices companies, doing market analysis, and applying Porter model measures to ensure that the best practices were being applied with best suppliers offering both top capability and staying power. Along the way, processes were dramatically simplified and personnel were liberated to do more productive, value-adding work.

The continual improvement process provides the supply team the structure necessary to create the consistency in approach demonstrated by Mellon. It begins with analysis of the customer's usage, value chain mapping, and developing a TCO model. These steps provide a comprehensive view of the current supply stream and its supporting processes.

A simple way to use the TCO model is to assign each supply-stream cost (see Figure 5-7) to one of the major cost categories of the TCO formula. Next, estimate the total percentage cost associated with each category, as follows:

A Sample of Estimated Percentages of
Total Cost in Each Cost Category

$$\text{TCO} = A + O + T + M + W + E - S$$
$$100\% = 25\% + 40\% + 10\% + 20\% + 5\% + 0\% - 0\%$$

Because the acquisition costs are known, the supply leader can compute the other cost categories algebraically. For example:

If x = Total cost of ownership (TCO), then

$$.25x \quad = \quad \text{Acquisition cost}$$
$$x \quad = \quad \frac{\text{Acquisition cost}}{.25}$$

or

$$\text{TCO} \quad = \quad \text{Acquisition cost} \div .25$$

Breaking TCO down into its component categories provides a basis for prioritizing improvement efforts. For example, if 40 percent of total cost is in the maintenance category, this would be a prime target for early improvement work.

As with value chain mapping, we recommend that this "scoping" exercise be developed with the supplier. The supplier often has other customer data on dimensions of cost and can quickly help to build a total cost view while beginning to share practices for improvement.

This scoping analysis creates the framework for the on-going work. It is where the "hard" supply management job of understanding the work behind each of the supply-stream steps begins: how it is ordered, delivered, used, maintained, prepared, salvaged; what its measures of use are; how others track its effectiveness.

The entire benchmarking process within the continual improvement work is aimed at securing knowledge of best industry practices and processes, along with specific measurement points for comparison with the current supply stream in your business.

The Supply Teams Improvement Plan will include a current and projected total cost model. This becomes the basis for supply stream effectiveness. Chapter 8 will cover the complete performance measures for supply management. But the total cost concept is pervasive.

Linking the Supplier's Value Chain to the Ultimate Customer

Market analysis, value chain mapping, and TCO are the vital concepts allowing you to link your supplier to your customers. As shown in Figure 5-9, linking the supplier's value chain to your ultimate customer's is a powerful way of using the collective resources of the supply base to meet your customer's needs. It also helps the supplier focus on your customer's needs. Some suppliers focus their resources on improving final products; others manage supporting, nonessential goods and services so that the key resources of the business can be focused on the customer.

Figure 5-9. Linking value chains.

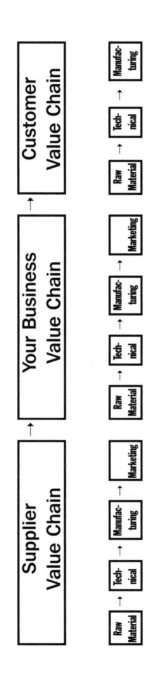

The Supply Management Skill Set

The shift from a transactional, task-filled purchasing role to a more strategic, problem-solving supply management role requires a new set of business, market, and financial skills (see Figure 5-10).

The supply management process will transform procurement buyers into supply managers, if supported with applied skill building, within two to three years, though results will begin to accrue almost immediately.

Figure 5-10. The supply management skill set.

- Market/industry analysis
- Supplier cost-analysis and cost-modeling
- Financial understanding of profit-and-loss statements and balance sheets
- Value chain mapping and work flow redesign
- Benchmarking and search for best practices
- Legal understanding for contract preparation
- Relationship management

Figure 5-11 depicts the changing role of the buyer as the transactional tasks are replaced with new supply management work. Chapter 8 discusses the specific steps and skills required to perform the supply management role.

Supply Management: The Benefits

The supply management process delivers three stages of cost and strategic/market benefits. As illustrated in Figure 5-12, the benefits of implementing these concepts are so reproducible that they almost qualify as new universal constants.

Figure 5-11. Changing role of the buyer.

Buyer Role		Supply Manager Role
Proceeds from procurement transaction focus: purchase, delivery, supplier payment	→	Creates customized material/service stream strategies
Focuses on audit perspective, follow-up, delivery, specifications	→	Manages supplier resources for continual improvement
Focuses on internal processes	→	Uses external benchmarking for best practices
Depends on internal service to provide supply	→	Links supplier and customer value chains

Figure 5-12. Supply management benefits.

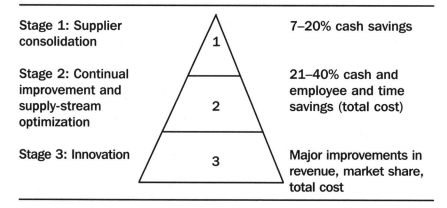

Stage 1: Supplier consolidation	1	7–20% cash savings
Stage 2: Continual improvement and supply-stream optimization	2	21–40% cash and employee and time savings (total cost)
Stage 3: Innovation	3	Major improvements in revenue, market share, total cost

1. *The supplier consolidation stage* rewards simple volume leverage with a 5–7 percent reduction in acquisition costs. (All the procurement initiatives work of the late 1980s and early 1990s was targeted at these quick benefits.)

If purchases for a given supply stream can be consolidated with "best suppliers" who at start-up can help to streamline certain practices and improve usage, the actual cash savings quickly move into double digits.

The supply teams most successful in generating cash rewards are those that select suppliers that will best optimize the total supply stream, obtaining the front end benefits of price leverage plus the far greater benefits of usage improvements almost immediately. When stage 1 and stage 2 begin to combine, it is not unusual to see first-year dollar savings of over 20 percent.

2. *The continual improvement stage* is, of course, where the harder work takes place: actually changing usage patterns, eliminating inventories, devising new product standards, standardizing application practices, training, and so on. Benefits accrue in cash and noncash terms (e.g., actual usage savings, employee time savings, lower inventories, lower system costs). This stage, however, is richest in rewards, which are limited only by the supply stream's ability to engage end users in making the required changes and contributing the necessary time. The key is measurement— quantitative and qualitative.

3. *The innovation stage* can occur at any time; it most definitely does not occur in a neat sequential step. En route to seeking opportunities for improvement, one often trips and falls over a chance for real innovation that was previously overlooked. The purpose of the innovation process is to periodically seek out all the hidden opportunities. When such innovation occurs, it creates major shifts in product

features or benefits that can generate new revenue for your business *or* so significantly change your manufacturing or development process as to substantially alter the product cost or dramatically shorten the time-to-market for new products. This happens within positive relationships between best suppliers and best customers.

Again, markets and technologies are changing every day. The supply management process is designed to guide the supply team through an ongoing evolution of improvement, marked by continuing changes in cost and functionality.

Of course, if your business has never been down this path at all, the potential benefits are huge. Aside from the tangible benefits in cash flow and profit margin, multiple strategic benefits for competitive advantage accrue to your business when it has successfully implemented supply management. Process innovations begin to aid the entire innovation cycle as it provides new features for the marketplace. These features and improved cost position are rewarded with increased market share and increased customer revenue.

The expected time from initiating the supply management process to reaping its benefits and rewards is short—three to six months to begin receiving cost benefits and one to two years to achieve the first round of market rewards. No other business process known today can deliver the size or impact of cash and market benefits within these time frames.

The Supply Community

When General Motors initiated its supplier consolidation process in the early 1990s, our participation in that effort gave us valuable insight into the supply community. Generally, the suppliers fell into three categories:

1. *Suppliers with clear competitive advantage in cost or product uniqueness.* These suppliers responded with the most comprehensive, professional descriptions of the marketplace, their business and product strategies, and information about their costs. Low-cost producers proudly displayed their P&Ls. Market leaders protected their profit information but willingly discussed cost components. In sum, these suppliers had nothing to hide and were on firm ground to add to customer value.

2. *Suppliers with declining competitive advantage and products comparable to other marketplace offerings.* These suppliers' responses were of the "sales" variety—the smoke and mirrors of repeating product features and benefits. They rarely could or would address the questions of strategy or cost. Their objective was to buy time, hoping this whole phase would pass by.

3. *Suppliers with questionable competitive advantage but acquainted with a senior officer in the business.* These suppliers attempted to circumvent the process altogether, relying on personal relationships to protect their supplier status. When questioned directly, they usually refused disclosure of any significant information.

At the end of the supplier consolidation process, the suppliers with the most competitive advantage were consistently among the short list of preferred suppliers. The choices were made on the basis of best leverage opportunities, of course, but special knowledge that suppliers could bring to bear on improving the total supply stream was also considered. It didn't take long for the preferred suppliers to figure out that if supplier consolidation were to become a national trend, they could turn their responses into a proactive marketing program and aggressively gain market share.

In fact, this is what began to happen. In the next five years, major consolidation occurred in every supply market, with big winners and losers. Almost without exception, the suppliers who chose to raise their hand ("Pick me! And let me describe how I can help you to optimize your supply-stream program!") had gained considerable market position. Companies such as Vallen Safety Supply, VWR Scientific, Calgon, and Corporate Express are still market leaders today because of the proactive approach they use to meet the new supply management challenges. They answered the *real* question: How can you enhance our competitive advantage?

Two years ago we met one electrical supplies distributor who was colocating a full-time engineer with each key customer to help standardize products and reduce inventories. By becoming more familiar with the customer's processes, the distributor was able to more effectively divert its resources to help solve customer problems.

Only recently we participated in a major supplier effort to consolidate providers of operating supplies. The customer's company was buying pipe, valves and fittings, electrical supplies, power transmissions, and operating supplies to support fifty-three locations through 5,000 suppliers. The company developed a very organized consolidation program and simultaneously engaged distributor suppliers in all four supply groups to discuss proposals for improved supply-stream processes. Again the responses were widely different and the proactive suppliers, prepared with a plan and backed with experience, shone like a headlight.

As a result the company went from 5,000 local suppliers

to a combination of eleven regional and national suppliers. It formed regional consortiums of four to five distributors, which began working together to develop shared processes for ordering, inventory, distribution, and information management.

We had the opportunity to participate in the kick-off meeting, attended by senior executives from all eleven suppliers. The suppliers without new contracts in hand had people already working at locations to develop inventory analysis, determine new pricing structures, and identify opportunities for product standardization. Quite a change in response from the GM supplier meetings!

Clearly not all suppliers are intimately familiar with supply management concepts and processes. However there is a marked shift in their openness and willingness to work with you to discuss more than buying and selling products, and it's important for you to have a clear understanding of supply management in order to benefit from their new willingness. When your organization initiates this process—or more likely, gets beyond the simple leverage phase—the supply community is ably prepared to respond. Suppliers are prepared not only to describe strategies and costs but to help to build process maps, devise new practice opportunities, *and* provide the resources for implementation in your business.

Summary

The supply management process is an ongoing learning process, not a tug-of-war to see who controls the buying decision or selects the supplier. It is aimed at installing a standardized mechanism for focusing people on the relevant priorities with the right buying strategies, thus enhancing the business's competitive position.

Furthermore, the supply management process helps you to quickly sort out which purchases are strategically significant and which are merely essential. For producers of plastics packaging, resin is a strategic resource. It is a vital component of the final product; office supplies are not. The two require different strategies and different criteria. Yet, the supply management process yields the most appropriate managing strategies for each.

Implementing the supply management process allows you to take a fresh look at your existing supply base. You can then begin a consolidation and leveraging program as the first stage in incorporating this process in each business function.

Once you consolidate your supplier base, the teams formed during this first stage focus their attention on working with the selected suppliers to drive the material/ service to the next generation of improvement and innovation in support of your company's competitive advantage.

As the supply process is implemented, the cost savings begin to accrue and the strategic benefits become visible. Early signs of these strategic benefits come from many areas:

- Cross-functional leaders begin reexamining the fundamental raw material mix and processing technologies.
- Market leaders begin rethinking product characteristics that can be made available with best innovation, technologies, and practices.
- Manufacturing leaders begin reexamining total material and service costs for entire business units, prioritizing these by *value-adding, essential,* or *non-essential* cost classifications.

The tangible benefits accrue from the new revenue generated from cost savings turned into increased profit margins and rising market share generated by product innovation.

As a strategic process, supply management affects all aspects of profitability. In doing so, it becomes a new platform for competitive advantage.

IMPLEMENTATION GUIDE

Key to leading a supply management initiative is familiarity with the key concepts and processes. The easiest way to remember these is to apply them to the products or services your business takes to the marketplace.

Market Analysis

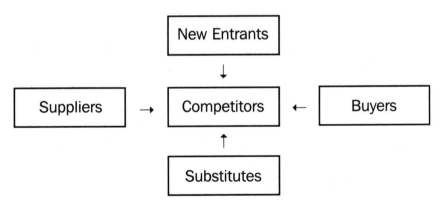

- Identify the product and industry you will use in this example.
- List your product/business as one of the competitors in the center box, labeled "Competitors."

- Identify other leading competitors. Can you identify the low-cost producer? The distinctive market leader?
- Identify major types of buyers (your customers). How do they make their buying decisions? What's important? Price? Features and functionality?
- Identify major suppliers to your industry. Types? Names?
- Identify possible new market entrants. Are these new global entrants? New technologies?
- Identify substitute products your customers could select.
- Who has the most leverage in the current market (who controls the price)? Competitors? Buyers? Suppliers?
- Are there likely new entrants or substitutes?
- What's the key to competitive advantage? Technology? Scale? Distribution? Cost?
- Who are the "best" top five competitors?
- Are you among these top five? If not, why not?
- You aren't a supplier. Or are you?

Value Chain Mapping

- Depict a simple flowchart, beginning with your customer's order for your product, showing all the steps necessary to manufacture or provide delivery, including your receipt and payment by your customer.
- Determine which steps are value-adding.
- Which steps could be eliminated or streamlined if the customer were willing?
- Do you know how the customer uses your product?
- Are there better ways for the customer to use your product that you haven't shared?

Total Cost of Ownership

- Is your business a manufacturing, assembly, or service business?
- What is the average price and the average inventory value for your product or service?
- The estimated total cost of ownership for your customer is:

  Manufacturing
business	4	x (Your product price) =
Assembly business	2	x (Your product price) =
Service business	1.33	x (Your product price) =

- Are you providing proposals to help your customer manage this *total cost?* What would you suggest?
- Remember, your prices are your customer's costs.

These are the three driving concepts that can help you to select a best supplier and engage it in creating strategies that improve your total supply stream. Clearly there are opportunities to share these same concepts with your customers. Is this how your customers think of you?

Finally, the following summarizes the supply management processes, their outcomes, and their benefits. These processes and concepts are the primary tools for the supply management process.

Supply Management
Core Processes

Procurement Process	Continual Improvement Process	Innovation Process
↓	↓	↓
To Select Best Suppliers With Most Competitive Advantage	To Optimize Supply-Stream Flow and Use	To Create Innovation in Customer Functionality
↓	↓	↓
Supplier Consolidation and Cost Savings	Cost Savings Employee Time Savings	Cost Improvement New Revenues

CHAPTER 6

How to Get Started

As you can see, supply management is a comprehensive business process to help you reexamine all purchased materials and services so that you can optimize the total cost of ownership. How then to begin? First, here's what *not* to do:

- Do not reorganize the procurement function.
- Do not send out an executive mandate, "There should be a supply management effort," and return to your duties.
- Do not send this book to your staff with a note, "Send me your thoughts."

Supply management requires executive leadership to set a course of action, create a forum for understanding, and engage the relevant people who will actually implement these processes and concepts. By definition, executive accountabilities include *setting direction, developing policies, specifying processes, building organizational skill,* and *removing barriers.*

Let us review a simple approach for engaging and mobilizing your organization to begin a comprehensive supply management process.

Setting Direction

The very first step is to internalize the idea that launching a new process is like a journey. You don't know all you need to know before you begin, but you start anyway with the expectation of certain rewards at the end and with this book as your map.

Launching new processes requires changing procedures, behavior, attitudes, beliefs, policies—many dimensions embedded within your organizational culture. Only executive leadership can signal a change in direction so that employees will know they are expected to deal with change. No matter how compelling the case for supply management and its outcomes and benefits, a broad signal to embrace this new process is imperative. Without this signal, small supply-stream efforts may start, but they will never achieve the momentum necessary to generate significant results.

Setting direction takes many forms, including a simple expression of "intent to pursue." A likely beginning is to assemble a forum of peers and key participants from purchasing, operations, business groups, Finance, and Law. Introduce the leading-edge "best practice" of supply management as a replacement for your current procurement process. Share the key concepts and benefits. Engage the group to help you design the ways and methods to take this work forward.

Finally, set an expectation for the magnitude of results you're seeking and a time frame for completion. For example, when we first were asked to become involved in a procurement initiative in our business, the direction was clear:

> *"Get us $100 million of invoice savings in three years."*

Having little idea of where to begin, at least we knew the magnitude of the sought-after solution and the rate of speed at which we needed to travel.

You, on the other hand, having been exposed to this concept and in a position to benefit from our learning, could rephrase the mandate something like this: "We must have a reduction of $100 million in our total costs and improve our competitive advantage at the same time. Examine supply opportunities. Look at key processes. It must be a sustaining initiative. I will be reviewing plans with you to ensure realization of the goal." Practically speaking, your merely creating this forum signals change and provides the opportunity for interested leaders to step forward.

The outcomes of this early forum should include a work plan to identify the usual what, who, how, and when.

Let's look at some real examples. At nearly the same time, a telecommunications giant in the Northeast and a large national banking and financial services holding company each recruited vice-presidents to realize strategic benefits in the purchase of goods and services. In both cases the word *strategic* had never before been used in the same sentence with the word *procurement*. Let's restate that: *Strategic* and *procurement* were probably not even used in the same reports.

Both companies buy in the billions-of-dollars category. Both are success stories, and they would be success stories if their purchases were only $10 million. Size did not create their success; in fact, it probably complicated it.

Both vice-presidents did the same things. Both began to see significant results in less than six months, results that were not clumsy slapdash panic attempts to show progress. The results were consistent with results seen in supply management efforts today, two years later. Both vice-presidents launched long-term situation analysis projects and expenditure data gathering, organization capability building, and communications campaigns. Concurrently, they blitzed accounts payable and general ledger data to identify a limited number of supply streams that could be determined by identifying suppliers from industries that are easily discernible by supplier name (e.g., Canon, Kodak, and Xerox in copiers; Sprint, AT&T, and MCI in telecommunications). After determining relatively large expenditures with multiple suppliers, then further determining that no consistently professional process beyond occasional bidding was in place for these goods and services, they identified the primary users. If there was a focal point or ownership by a particular stakeholder group, so much the better.

Representatives of these groups at the decision-making level were gathered and given an overview of supply management, the value of teams (of which they were about to become members), and the opportunity the particular supply stream presented.

The best of the existing procurement group were enlisted to work the project. Financial analysis capability was borrowed from the financial group. This not only provided instant help before analysts could be hired but also brought credibility to the numbers. If either of these resources is not available, consultants can supplement as required. It is important that the procurement head control the direction and not lose control of the effort to an outside organization. Remember, the purpose is to establish supply management as a long-term strategy, establishing knowledge and process, not to take some quickly leveraged price benefits and run, as is often the case with some outside companies.

Within the first five months, the bank holding company had cut its copier suppliers from seven to one, had taken annual expenditures down by $3.5 million, had shifted total administration to the supplier, which had the expertise, eliminated the need to warehouse supplies, and shifted from hundreds of paper invoices each month to a single summary electronic bill. In addition, significant capital was freed by the shift to a cost-per-copy arrangement.

This success became a vehicle to publicize supply management and to begin to educate senior management about the value of taking the concept across the board, from health care to legal services to advertising agencies. It also provided a forum to explain what senior management "support" is. There's more on this later in this chapter, but for now:

■ It is *not* specific mandates to all the players about what they must do. That will only cause resentment and sabotage.

■ It is understanding the concept and potential of supply management and offering visible and verbal support to the supply management leaders and to the teams they are and will be working with, letting the organization know that this is one of the corporate six priorities (or whatever the number is). It also involves establishing real marketing communications to establish awareness of new supply-stream benefits.

Back to the two companies and early successes.

The bank holding company went on to simultaneously run business-segment and corporatewide supply-stream projects, complete with process mapping of the acquisition and usage processes and with quarterly joint performance evaluations to ensure continual improvement.

The telecommunications company's tactics were similar. The chairman was engaged in the process, which became part of the corporate strategy. The participation and pace were dramatic. Needs presented themselves: fleet management, cabinet doors, a complex information system, collection agency contracts. These were not ideally constructed material streams. They were things that needed to be bought, contracts that needed to be renewed. The company introduced cross-functional teams and found "one plus one equals three": The users understood the requirements and the supply managers understood the process. The supply teams did thorough market research to identify the best companies. The old process would not have accomplished that; existing contracts would likely have been renewed. The teams learned by research and benchmarking that the company's costs for collection were higher than industry norms and its collections rates lower. Team members decided to focus on their core business in these instances and work together to identify world-class suppliers that could bring "new expertise to the table." They also expanded the process to cover all of the company, not just particular segments. The focused approach didn't cost time—it saved time. The team had direction. True cost savings were in the double digits. Measurable quality increased. New ideas and competitive advantage resulted. The teams felt confident. The capable suppliers were rewarded. All of this was done early in the process of developing data, building capability in the organization, and so on. A few focused people with even limited training can produce real and lasting results with leadership and backing. Just do it!

Developing Policies

The good news is that at this stage it's too early to define new policies. The larger issue is that you will quickly be met with requests for change that is outside your current policies. Specific policies that will be influenced by the supply management process include:

- Current policies that specify guidelines for customers who are also suppliers
- Audit and control policies for payments
- Policies for legal agreements and contracts
- Ethics policies for supplier-provided gifts and entertainment
- Expense policies
- Approval and spending policies, including authorization limits

The point is not to let these current policies become a barrier for new supply-stream solutions as they are developed. Rather, set a tone of encouragement for new solutions and indicate a willingness to examine new benefits. These policies can be modified at a later date.

Most of the administrative, non-value-adding procedures and tasks that flood the workplace are the direct result of the need to support some current corporate policy, as though to demonstrate behavior consistent with the company's stone tablet of rules.

The transactional reengineering of the procurement process alone will require the elimination of many of these procedures and tasks. This is not to say you should give up "controls" or "ethics" or adherence to "legal doctrine." Rather, you will refine policies and utilize broad processes to create consistent applications.

Specifying Processes

The supply management approach guides supply leaders through the three core processes of procurement, continual improvement, and innovation, described in more detail in Chapter 8. Rather than spending time designing new processes to guide procurement and improvement actions, we recommend that you specify that "these core processes are to be used to optimize all supply streams."

All too often, as businesses embark on a mission of improvement, the whole burst of front-end human energy is spent "designing the process." This occurs only after mission leaders have turned "admiring the problem" into an art form. We believe this is one of the reasons so many "new initiatives" run out of steam—they are not focused on getting something done. The concepts in this book are implementation tools, meant to help you create tangible benefits quickly. So why waste time "organizing" to get started? The ingredients for success are leadership and a few motivated supply managers.

The ultimate value for your business will never derive from creating the perfect process, nor from developing the perfect form. It will arise in great waves from unleashing people to implement for a common goal. So hand them the processes and get on with it.

Building Organizational Skill

An often-used model for creating total organizational skill is captured in the motto, Skill, will, and access, the keys to unleashing your organization. We've always liked this simple tool, because it's such a straightforward reminder of the executive's accountabilities.

Simply:

- For *skill,* do the people selected to implement these new tasks have the functional skills to complete the work?

- For *will*, have you created an environment wherein the people believe they can succeed and so are motivated to perform?
- For *access*, have you removed barriers or constraints that might keep your team from completing this new work?

In this case the supply leaders in fact acquire some new functional skills—at minimum in market analysis, value chain mapping, and total cost of ownership, as well as in project management. Organizational development experts have concluded that on-the-job skill building is the most effective way to transfer learning. When you create an environment where individuals can immediately apply these concepts to a given supply stream, several benefits occur, including the following:

- The supply team actually completes new work. This work might result in a plan to consolidate suppliers or in an actual value chain map analysis along with an improvement plan.
- The supply team is better able to understand the concepts in relation to their individual work accountabilities and specific supply streams.
- This early work creates immediate tangible results. So, in as little as two to three months' time, the supply participants receive tangible reinforcement of their learning.

A simple way to begin is to identify a cross section of supply streams as a pilot supply management effort. Draft the current supply/procurement leaders and have them identify a team of relevant users and functional experts.

Ask your procurement leader to provide an on-site skill building session for these teams, making certain that the outcomes are directed at actual implementation.

This launch training session should include five to six supply teams, with four to six people per team. The training session and subsequent work will create a likely forum for shared learning that can be translated across other supply streams. And the process begins.

Specific curricula for skill building and mechanisms that can be used to capture ongoing learning are discussed in Chapter 8.

Removing Barriers

No matter how compelling your direction, or how motivated the new supply teams, your leadership will be necessary to open doors to change, because these supply teams are creating cross-functional mechanisms. Although cross-functional teams are not new, in most companies they most likely have not tried to make purchasing decisions for large communities of users, nor have they tried to change product, service, or usage patterns.

The "not invented here" syndrome so prevalent in functional operations will be the main operating barrier as these teams roll forward their implementation. However, purchasing, accounts payable, business management, and legal personnel can be great naysayers, too, as new ordering, payment, accounting, and contractual programs are proposed.

Obviously, every problem can't rise to the top of the organization. However, you can begin to create organizational forums for resolving differences, setting priorities, and reinforcing the overall direction. These mechanisms, in conjunction with continued communications about the supply management initiative, will eventually wear down the inertia to change. Chapters 8 and 10 deal with specific mechanisms and communications approaches as further weapons for your leadership arsenal.

At the least, you should visibly acknowledge the anticipated barriers and encourage cooperation for new thinking and approaches. As results begin to accrue, visibly share learning and recognize results with a large part of the organization. It will be clear that the new values are change, risk, and immediacy of results. Not a bad beginning.

Finally, you will need to determine who within the organization will be the ultimate supply management leader. This certainly can be the current procurement leader if this individual has an enlightened understanding of the opportunity and the leadership capabilities to pull it off. In many cases these competencies do reside in your current procurement and supply leaders, but they are held captive in their functional roles. In other cases this represents the opportunity for new leadership, often from outside procurement. Leaders with operations or business experience can quickly seize the logic of the supply management concepts. Unencumbered by current procurement procedures and processes, they will be eager to start with a clean slate to create a new order of things.

We can attest personally to this approach. Whomever you choose as the supply management leader must embrace the purpose and goals of this approach and have the motivation and capabilities to implement the complete program.

With these few planks in place, you are ready to begin.

Potential Roadblocks

There are clearly roadblocks to implementing the supply management process, like any process or initiative requiring behavioral change. However, they are of the "garden variety" of organizational resistance and all can be overcome with a good executive implementation effort. The most frequent roadblocks that must be dealt with include those in Figure 6-1.

Figure 6-1. Five roadblocks to change.

---

1. Lack of common understanding of direction and goals
2. Protectiveness of functional or individual turf
3. Leadership voids
4. Lack of functional skills
5. Lack of time and priority

■ *Lack of common understanding of direction and goals.* In short, organizations need a clear understanding of what they are trying to achieve. You should, "Write it—speak it—say it again." The communication of the purpose, goals, timing, expected benefits, impacts simply cannot be expressed often enough. The purpose of an ongoing communication plan is continual reinforcement of this direction. Your direction cannot be a one-time policy statement or meeting. All participants and affected employees need a "heads-up" call to change. The best plan is to deliver this clarity early and throughout the life of the supply management process.

■ *Protectiveness of functional or individual turf.* Turf, pure and simple, is always a tough barrier. The key to removing this barrier is to include the functional leaders in the plans and mechanisms for guiding this change.

Ideally, these functions are part of the realm of your peers and they can participate in the leadership forum to set this direction. If the supply team includes these functional representatives, it helps to build the credibility for the overall market strategy and the planned change.

At the end of the day, however, leadership messages about the greater good may not be enough. Intervention will be necessary to create some optimum supply-stream strategy. We recommend it be swift and visible. This will set the tone and help to defer or eliminate the turf barrier.

■ *Leadership voids.* Leadership voids at any level will delay and many times derail change initiatives. So, staffing a few of the key leadership roles early on, in addition to selecting the overall supply management leader, will help ensure that you have enough capable people to make this happen.

It's been our experience that, as you invite people to this new process, natural leaders step forward and latent leaders bloom. We have never seen an organization that couldn't implement supply management because of lack of enough supply-stream leaders. The failed attempts were a result of poor leaders in more senior roles, including the executive level. We aren't kidding about the need for strong executive leadership, but strong functional leadership is critical too.

■ *Lack of functional skills.* Clearly, setting people on a new course without a map or proven tools is pointless. The decision to invest in reskilling supply managers and team participants needs to be a part of the early implementation plan. Without it you will fail.

■ *Lack of time and priority.* Even if the most compelling supply-stream plan is brought forth, with promise of huge dollar savings, there must be agreement to implement the actual change. All of the supply-stream plans will cause some change. For some end users there will be new suppliers, new products, new usage methods, new ordering methods, and so on. The users will need the permission and possible direction from their functional or business leaders to include this work in their operating priorities.

Longer-term shared annual goals and incentives can serve to facilitate the continual improvement of the supply management process and its outputs. At the beginning, however, unless there is a prescription for integrating this work as a priority and allocating the necessary time to it, it will be among the last tasks completed and benefits will be delayed.

One way to think about this roadblock is to remember that every day you spend dollars for materials and services. So every day you delay optimizing, you leave "on the table" dollar benefits that otherwise could be added to your bottom line. No other short-term improvement projects will have as great an impact on your business profitability as these supply-stream benefits. Adjusting priorities to implement the supply management process will be well worth the effort.

IMPLEMENTATION GUIDE

Chapter 5 describes the key processes and concepts that compose the supply management process. The functional leaders within your organization will develop the expert competencies over time to use these processes to optimize your supply streams.

The essential leadership work at this stage is to get them started. This is a function of setting direction and removing roadblocks.

A quick checklist of suggested actions follows.

Getting Started

Setting direction	■ Introduce supply management to a cross-functional forum of peers and other leaders.
	■ Share expected benefits and keys to success.
	■ Engage the team in developing direction and key roles.
	■ Be visible and clear about expectations and goals.
Developing policies	■ Encourage change and new thinking.
	■ Be willing to intervene to make policy issue exceptions.
	■ Don't stay married to policies as they are written today.
Specifying process	■ Specify the use of core supply management processes for all supply streams.
Building organizational skills	■ Create pilot supply teams, at least five.
	■ Provide on-the-job skill building with new supply management concepts.
	■ Create a forum to share actual results.
	■ Popularize results and recognize work.

Removing barriers	■ Create cross-functional leadership teams to set priorities and remove barriers.
	■ Be open to providing support and overturning functional barriers.
	■ Be swift.

Potential Roadblock Busters

Lack of common understanding	■ Set purpose, goals, and expectations visibly.
	■ Communicate, communicate, communicate.
	■ Build comprehensive communication plan to reinforce messages.
Turf protectionism	■ Lead by example; recognize and reward cooperation and barrier removal.
Leadership voids	■ Identify key leaders and functions and capability to support roles.
	■ Fill/compensate for executive voids.
Lack of functional skills	■ Develop/implement ongoing skill building for functional concepts or processes.
Lack of time and priority	■ Integrate goals into functional priorities.
	■ Set tone and recognize/ reward results.

What should be self-evident is frequently lost in the complexity of experiencing new concepts and their benefits. No single implementation step is as critical to the success of this process as senior executives setting direction and staying the course.

CHAPTER 7

Supply-Stream Strategies: Classification and Development

We want to be sure that we beat one point to death: This isn't about buying stuff; it's about managing the stuff you buy. This shift in focus provides the grist for new sources of competitive advantage.

The entire purpose of developing individual strategies to manage the acquisition *and* the use of purchased materials and services is simply to ensure that your business maximizes the value of its investment. Several facts about purchased materials and services drive a need for these strategies and bear repeating:

■ The purchase price alone represents only, on average, 25–40 percent of the total cost of ownership. Other costs include waste in use, maintenance costs, and training costs.

■ Understanding the actual usage practices for a material or service provides the largest opportunity for maximizing value. Yet, organizations rarely focus on securing these best practices from leading suppliers. The result is waste in material, service time, or, even worse, employee time.

■ The actual purchase and delivery process itself represents a second opportunity for eliminating wasted steps and maximizing value for both you and your suppliers. These benefits come from reducing transactional and handling costs, eliminating inventories, and reducing cycle times.

■ The supply management core processes (procurement, continual improvement, and innovation) are designed to seek out suppliers with best practices and the resources to help you optimize use of a purchased material or service and its total cost.

■ Because the predominant value for a business accrues after the purchase, new effort must be applied to ensure that the supplier focuses its resources on securing this value. This management activity cannot be undertaken for an infinite number of suppliers. Industry benchmarks indicate that leading-edge large corporate organizations consolidate their supplier base to about 1,000 total suppliers, with 250–350 preferred key supplier relationships. This supplier consolidation requirement provides the opportunity to rethink a whole new platform of preferred supplier relationships. In this way, you can access the various market segments to source purchased materials and services in search of the "best" suppliers. Furthermore, by understanding supplier costs, you can leverage the volume with suppliers who have the best cost structures, thereby producing the lowest possible ultimate pricing.

■ You can maximize opportunities for competitive advantage only by drawing on a cadre of suppliers with proven competitive market positions, augmented by leading-edge practices and cost structures.

■ The combination of these strategies to manage the acquisition and the use of purchased materials and services will yield 10–20 percent in immediate acquisition price savings for each material/service stream consolidated. *Simple supplier bidding processes will not deliver this magnitude of savings.*

In Chapter 2 we discussed the scope and activities of the differences between the traditional purchasing function and those of the supply management process. We made clear that supply management is a strategic endeavor that not only extends from the very beginning of a business development cycle through the point of value received but also spans the breadth of a company's functions. Whether the subject is codevelopment of a critical aircraft engine module by means of a concurrent engineering arrangement with a supply partner or managing a supply relationship for consolidated acquisition and use of office products on a national scale, the elements are the same. Resources, time to implement, and scale of benefits may differ, but the philosophy and critical elements to be addressed are nearly identical.

Now before we turn to developing managing strategies for supply chains, it's helpful to be sure we know what problem we're trying to solve. The strategy development phase of supply management is not a "one size fits all" practice. Rather, it begins by defining the types of strategies we want to create for a purchased material or service.

This is the work of business executives and leaders. Supply management and/or procurement professionals will develop the actual strategies for each material stream, but categorizing each stream according to its relative strategic importance to the total business, determining its priority, and providing the needed overall support of the effort are the job of executive management.

Supply-Stream Classification

Maximizing the value of each supply stream requires selecting the "best suppliers" and developing customized strategies for each supply stream. Some general classifications can be made to assist the supply manager in strategy development. These classifications are based on two factors:

1. The role of the purchased material/service in your business's value chain. Is it core to creating value for customers? Or does it serve only to support the business infrastructure?

2. Whether your business requires a customized product/service or can use available market offerings.

This classification effort can provide insights into the market (e.g., trailing-edge versus leading-edge technology, low-cost producer versus distinctive market leader) and the implications for developing supply management strategies. This classification *is not* intended to create a hierarchy of purchased materials and services, nor is it intended to prioritize the importance of supply streams. A $5 million transportation buy requires as careful supply chain planning as a $5 million software investment.

Strategy Development

Every supply stream requires its own carefully developed management strategy because each stream has different requirements, customers, markets, suppliers, and other variables. The challenge for procurement leaders is how to organize an approach and decide which part of the process to standardize. In most procurement processes the supplier selection process is standardized to such finite, cumbersome levels that the buyer and internal user have no freedom or time to explore market opportunities. Furthermore, this approach tends to treat all supply streams—big or small, strategic or nonstrategic, national or local—in the same way.

The supply strategy development process begins by engaging internal users in the requirement description phase *and* in the market analysis process in order to search out the optimal supplier for a given requirement. This correct matching can occur only if you understand the role each purchased material or service plays in supporting your business goals.

Classification and Development Guidelines

The following classification and development guidelines have been developed to help you categorize your purchases and to determine their supply strategy requirements.

Each supplier consolidation and purchase effort for a business should begin by answering two questions:

1. Does the purchased material or service relate *directly* to the way a business creates value for its customers (does it have customer focus)?
2. Does the market solution require a *customized* or *standard* product or service? (What is your market focus?)

Answers to these questions help the supply management team organize the many material and service streams into the groupings shown in Figure 7-1. The quadrants of Figure 7-1 are in no way hierarchical. There is no intent to indicate that one is more important than another. The numbers assigned to each are simply a means to facilitate identification of the correct strategy and to identify the right people to work on supply-stream development. It is certainly true that there will likely be more senior management involvement in quadrant 2 because it represents not only a material or service that contributes to a core part of the business but one that must be customized as well, and in all probability is part of an offering that distinguishes a company in the marketplace.

Figure 7-1. Supply stream classification.

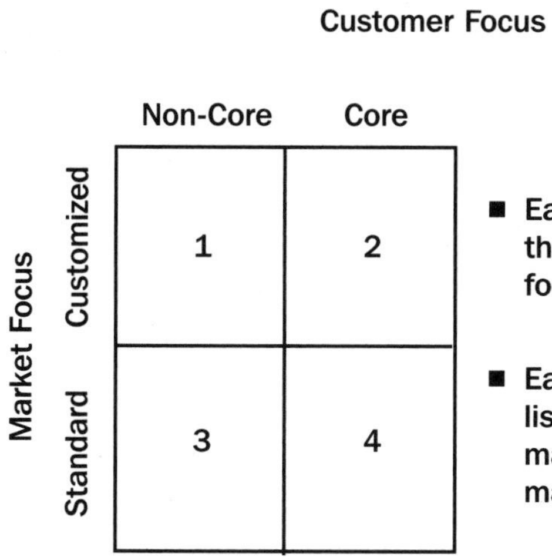

Customer Focus

	Non-Core	Core
Customized	1	2
Standard	3	4

Market Focus

- Each quadrant represents the combination of possible focuses.

- Each quadrant triggers a list of implications for the market search and the managing strategies.

Quadrant 1: Non-Core/Customized Purchases

Table 7-1 provides the characteristics and implications of products and services belonging in the non-core/customized quadrant (quadrant 1).

Table 7-1. Characteristics and implications of quadrant 1 (non-core/customized).

Description	This classification generally applies to products and services that do not directly provide value to the end customer but contribute significant supporting capability. Examples include cost-effective data processing centers, high-technology maintenance, surveillance systems, and specialized technology and skills to support cost-effective functionality.
Target supplier characteristics	Typically, supply managers sourcing these products or services search the market for the best, specialized, lowest-cost, most-efficient, and most-effective specialized solutions. Suppliers with leading-edge low-cost processes, systems, features, and benefits are sought out to improve business operations.
Supply management process focus	The supply manager uses primarily the procurement and continual improvement processes to select low-cost providers and optimize usage practices.
Key considerations	Frequently, quadrant 1 includes current products and services that have been previously "overspecified." Items in this classification must meet the criterion: Do we need customized features and functionality?

Quadrant 2: Core/Customized Purchases

Table 7-2 provides the characteristics and implications of products and services in the core/customized quadrant (quadrant 2).

Table 7-2. Characteristics and implications of quadrant 2 (core/customized).

Description	This classification applies to products and services that directly create value for the end customer. These goods and services create customized special features, attributes, and benefits in a business's products and services. Examples include specialized software, critical raw materials, and professional skills to design new services and products.
Target supplier characteristics	Supply managers for these products and services search the market for distinctive products, services, and technologies through suppliers that are leaders in the distinctive market segment.
Supply management process focus	The supply manager uses primarily the procurement and innovation processes to select innovation leaders, install leading-edge usage practices, and continually look for innovation features and attributes.
Key considerations	Suppliers of this classification provide customized value-added services to reduce cycle time in product development programs. As a result, they are strategic partners in creating competitive advantage for their respective businesses.

Quadrant 3: Non-Core/Standard Purchases

Table 7-3 provides the characteristics and implications for products and services in the non-core/standard quadrant (quadrant 3).

Table 7-3. Characteristics and implications of quadrant 3 (non-core/standard).

Description	This classification applies to products and services that are essential to support the business infrastructure but do not relate or provide value to the end customer. Examples include office supplies, maintenance tools and services, travel services, leased cars, furniture, building maintenance, and services. These items all tend to have the high transaction costs associated with frequently purchased items.
Target supplier characteristics	Typically, supply managers sourcing these products and services search the market for turnkey lowest-cost solutions, wherein the supplier frequently manages the entire provision stream in addition to supplying the specific product or service.
Supply management process focus	The supply manager uses primarily the procurement process to identify market leaders with lowest cost and self-managing continual improvement processes.
Key considerations	Supply managers work with these types of suppliers to provide a standard array of products and services for all internal customers and locations. The key value is derived from standardizing the offerings and streamlining or removing the access process. Opportunities exist for outsourcing internal tasks and procedures.

Quadrant 4: Core/Standard Purchases

Table 7-4 provides the characteristics and implications for products and services in the core/standard quadrant (quadrant 4).

Table 7-4. Characteristics and implications of quadrant 4 (core/standard).

Description	This classification applies to products and services that create value for the end customer but require only leading-edge market solutions that do not need to be customized exclusively for a business. These include professional services, switching systems, software, packaging systems, and marketing support services.
Target supplier characteristics	Supply managers search the market for distinctive market leaders with established positions and demonstrated competitive advantage in their products and services. They frequently provide best-operating and best-usage practices to improve effectiveness in use and reduce cycle time to market.
Supply management process focus	The supply manager uses primarily the procurement and continual improvement processes to seek out distinctive market leaders and install leading-edge practices. The innovation process is frequently used to track distinctive segment change.
Key considerations	Suppliers provide products, services, and practices at the leading edge of capability and are key to a business's competitive advantage by reducing cycle time to market. This market segment continually changes.

Table 7-5 summarizes the supply strategy characteristics of each classification quadrant. It is provided to help the supply manager:

- Define product and service stream requirements.
- Identify strategic questions for leading supplier organizations.
- Select managing processes.
- Engage relevant business resources.

The remainder of the supply strategy should be customized to meet the needs of individual business leaders or locations.

Table 7-5 serves as an excellent wallet card version of the guidelines for classifying purchased goods and services. It serves as a strategy development checklist for both process practitioners and executive management. If you know, for example, that a service or product has been classified as quadrant 1 and thus should be sourced with a low-cost provider but you see that the recommended supplier is a distinctive or innovation leader, this should sound an alarm: Either an error has been made or over time specifications have ballooned to require the capability of a more innovative supplier. This warning suggests an immediate review of the specifications to permit use of a low-cost source.

This approach represents best industry practice for engaging suppliers and developing supply chain strategies to manage the total cost of ownership.

The features and characteristics column in Table 7-5 highlights the supply strategy questions to be addressed after you have determined the role of a purchased material or service in your business. These features describe the suppliers of the purchased materials and services and their business strategies and capabilities. Management focus on these questions will help you and your suppliers to

Table 7-5. Classification and strategy implications of purchases.

Supplier Features and Management Characteristics	Material/Service Classification			
	Non-Core/ Customized 1	Core/ Customized 2	Non-Core Standard 3	Core Standard 4
Production Features				
1. Customized or standard	Customized	Customized	Standard	Standard
2. Distinctive provider or low-cost provider	Low-cost	Innovative leader/ distinctive leader	Low-cost	Distinctive leader
3. Supply-stream management requirements	Leading-edge processes for supplier and customer management	No supplier management required	Requires complete supplier management	Leading-edge processes for supplier and customer management
4. Central or local implementation strategy*	Local	Local	Central	Local
5. Risk	Medium	High	Low	Medium
6. Technology life cycle	Trailing edge	Leading edge	Trailing edge	Leading edge

(continues)

Table 7-5. (continued)
Supply Management
Process Characteristics

7. Procurement process	X	X	X	X
Continual improvement process	X	X	X	X
Innovation process		X		X
8. Supply management skill required	Medium	Highest	Introductory to medium	Medium to high
9. Supply chain process leadership	Business leader and supplier	Business leader, traditional role	Supplier, lead role	Business leader and supplier
10. Typical strategy opportunities	Respecify requirements to trailing edge	Improve cycle time Consolidate gains	Standardized processes and products for essential products and services	Select best provider Implement best practices
11. Key benefits	Cash costs Total cost	Revenue and profit	Cash costs Total cost Employee time	Cash costs Total cost

*Local means specific business unit or branch location.   © 1996 Sharon L. Robbins Supply Management Consulting.

develop appropriate strategies for your purchased materials and services.

Supplier Features and Management Characteristics

1. *Customized or standard products or services.* *Customized products* might refer to unique designs or a special tooling requirement. *Customized services* could be unique organizations or skills to perform functions in a special way or to yield a particularly low cost or unique capability. *Standard products* are off-the-shelf products or services. These terms refer to the method of producing, not to the cost or the distinctive characteristic of the provider.

You should ask whether or not the services or goods you purchase *must* be customized to meet your customer needs. Does your business *need* to spend the extra money for this customization? Must you have an end product with special features? Can you find this capability in an existing product offering?

2. *Distinctive provider or low-cost provider.* A *distinctive provider* is a supplier with a design, service, or product that is not available from anyone else. The product or service may be patented or copyrighted and presumably has extra value because of its unique design, appeal, or functionality. A *low-cost provider* is a supplier with the lowest cost in its industry or market segment.

The key question you need to answer is whether you need unique features or you need adequate features at the best, lowest cost? Is cost or product/service innovation more critical to your business success?

3. *Supply-stream management requirements.* Do you need to manage the entire supply-stream process, or can the supplier manage this process on your behalf? Quadrant 1, for example, indicates that "leading-edge processes" are

required because in all likelihood you will be asking the supplier to provide highly efficient practices and to manage this portion of the process on your behalf. In a quadrant 2 scenario, you would want to lead and manage completely those purchases that are critical to your success. Quadrant 3 cases would require the supplier to manage the complete supply chain process; in essence, this is the strategy for an outsourcing requirement. Quadrant 4 items would almost certainly benefit from a supplier offering leading-edge practices. It is important that the provider have a better capability than you for handling the acquisition and method of use of the purchased items. Can the provider do this for less cost? Can the supplier provide any synergies by taking this responsibility? Start by asking if there is a reason that you cannot delegate this to the provider. Seldom is this type of material or service a critical need that should be completely managed by your company and its employees.

4. *Central or local implementation strategy.* Do you require a national or global implementation strategy or one that must be customized for a specific plant or location? All of these supply processes will have a common strategy. However, the implementation plans may vary according to local needs. Virtually every non-core category will be implemented with the same provider in the same way nationwide. Some core services and products will have a local flavor, and there may be reasons to implement locally in different ways. This may require different suppliers. For example, an air travel strategy would be implemented at a global or national level with one or two main suppliers. Maintenance repair and operating supplies (MRO) strategies, however, tend to require local implementation with local suppliers. Don't worry about implementation differences; just be sure you are aware of what strategy is indi-

cated and be comfortable that you have captured the appropriate synergies and economies of scale.

5. *Risk.* Here *risk* refers to the importance of the purchase to the business or to the level of risk attendant in the implementation of a given supply stream. That risk is there, regardless of the method of design or purchase, but by classifying and grouping materials and services, you have a means to highlight and direct the right level of attention and resources to high-risk areas. This will help to ensure that you are doing the right level of strategy planning for all supply streams. Do you understand the risks to the company? Has the team dealt with them appropriately? Do your suppliers have plans to help you manage these risks? Are you spending too much time in planning costs to avoid minimal risk?

6. *Technology life cycle.* Do you need leading-edge or trailing-edge technology solutions? Leading-edge offerings cost more. Are these values important to your customers? From the Porter model (see Chapter 5) this characteristic refers simply to the life cycle stage of a particular supply-stream product or service, and its determination helps in the development of a supply-stream strategy, as well as in supplier selection. Refer to the Porter model and make sure your team understands clearly where a particular product is in its life cycle and that you are getting the appropriate customer value for selecting the leading edge or the appropriate cost reductions if you have selected the trailing edge.

7. *Core processes.* The core processes are designed to achieve a continuum of benefits throughout the course of the supply stream, from procurement leverage, through a continual improvement phase, to breakthrough or innovative solutions. It is not difficult to move through the first two phases concurrently, as has been demonstrated by sev-

eral companies, but it is also clear that not all classes of supply streams lend themselves to significant benefits in each
of these processes. Supply leaders will use a different balance of these processes depending on the role of a purchased material or service in the business.

A quadrant 1 situation would suggest procurement
leverage cost benefits and the opportunity to continually
improve the way the products are used. Both processes will
continue to reduce total costs. Innovative breakthroughs
for materials/services in this category are possible but not
expected or sought after, other than for significant improvements in cost or effectiveness in use.

In quadrant 4 cases, on the other hand, all three
processes are used to maximize value while searching for
the next level of innovation.

8. *Supply management skills.* Different levels of supply
management skills are required to manage these different
categories of purchases. For example, these skill differences
are evident for office products (quadrant 3) and critical
supplies (quadrant 2), where the risk is high. Lower skill
levels are sufficient for low-risk, market standard purchases. Higher skill levels are required for larger purchase
streams with higher risks and more need for continual improvement and innovation.

9. *Supply chain leadership.* Leadership requirements for
the supply management process are a function of the criti-
cality of the stream to the business. Strong business leader
involvement is necessary for core products and services
with customized features (quadrant 2); suppliers and supply managers can handle the requirements for support
products and services (quadrant 3).

Do your supply management leaders understand their
roles? Where is business management taking or sharing a

supply leadership role? Do your leaders understand that this process is part of their new business planning and embedded in company operations? Do they embrace this concept and see the appropriate link to your customers?

10. *Strategy opportunities.* The typical supply strategy opportunities are explicit in Table 7-5, and opportunities for customer engagement are apparent. The larger point here is to continually ask whether you are capturing strategic benefits from continual improvement and innovation or you are merely pursuing another cost reduction goal.

11. *Key benefits.* The key benefits are the essential rewards expected from the core processes, but specific management checks are required to be sure these cost benefits are captured and that revenue enhancements (quadrant 2) and saved employee time (quadrant 3) are planned for and realized. Are you sure your planned benefits are realistic? Are there specific criteria to measure these benefits?

Applying the Strategy Classification and Development Guidelines

The classification and development guidelines for supply-stream strategy will help you to develop the appropriate supplier strategies for any purchased material or service. Further examples of strategies and outcomes for the major classification groups follow.

Strategies for Non-Core/Customized Materials and Services

One of the first things you might wish to do after classifying your purchase expenditures is to review purchases in the non-core/customized category. These purchases may be likely candidates for standardization and simplification. Often, non-core purchases that require customized features have been "overspecified" to meet an earlier technical standard. A reassessment of the current marketplace might indicate whether or not an opportunity exists to change to a standard offering or approach.

Payroll centers and systems and customer service telephone centers are examples of standard comprehensive service offerings. Other examples include a variety of production materials, such as wiring in electrical assemblies, plating compounds, insulation, fasteners, screws, and clips. Myriad components offer opportunities to standardize and consolidate sourcing. Non-core/customized purchases provide one of your largest opportunities to simplify and standardize a major portion of the total purchase stream.

Legacy information systems are a perfect example of this category of purchases. Typically, these are customized systems that continue to need ongoing software design maintenance and support each year simply because they are there. Xerox has led the way among large corporations in outsourcing its legacy information systems, retaining in-house development staff only for new strategic customer or business systems. In Xerox's case, the outsourcing process began with benchmarking other sourced service successes and conducting comprehensive market analysis. By reviewing both successes and failures of other companies, Xerox created an up-to-date market model that identifies the technology leader and the low-cost providers, those who can best explain how to control the total cost structure.

Analysis of supplier alternatives led Xerox and others to conclude that there were other companies that could better manage these systems, particularly since such systems were in those companies' core businesses.

Yet another example of sourcing opportunities for non-core purchases is a private fleet and its supporting operations. Recently, a large service provider began to reexamine its fleet operations, which included 18,000 vehicles, 300 garages, and 350 employees. Management was trying to determine whether or not company operations were the right size and in the right location. Although its fleet operations were not core to the competitive advantage of this business, they were a unique and important support function. Unfortunately, the cost of this function was increasing year after year.

A comprehensive market review turned up suppliers that could provide turnkey fleet service with better total cost and a promise to improve costs by 10 percent per year for the next three years. Clearly, fleet service is the core of the new supplier's business. The supplier would have systems and processes to manage size, location, and every other dimension of cost and service better than its customers.

The key for supply strategies for non-core/customized materials and services is to understand the role of the purchase stream in your business and to examine other marketplace alternatives for securing the lowest total cost.

Strategies for Core/Customized Materials and Services

Core/customized materials and services are essential to how your business creates value for its customers. The strategies for these materials and services are all aimed at finding the best features and value and finding them faster than your competitors. A telecommunications company, for example, succeeds or fails on being first with distinctive software features for switching systems that create new customer revenue opportunities. Other examples are special essences for perfumes, distinctive packaging, and so on.

The path to creating these strategies begins in the same way as for all supply streams: benchmarking and industry analysis to create a Porter model of supply alternatives (see Chapter 5). These are supply streams of such critical importance to creating added value that business leaders generally want to manage the supply chain usage directly. The primary strategies for these types of purchases are to locate the very best supplier capability and to create usage methods that incorporate leading-edge or even break-through practices.

The key for supply strategies for core/customized materials and services is to have the supply leaders focus on continual searches for innovation in form and usage in order to provide a consistent stream of new opportunities to build competitive advantage.

Strategies for Non-Core/Standard Materials and Services

Non-core/standard items are your commodities. The potential to enhance overall business competitive advantage comes from seeking the lowest-cost turnkey supplier strategies to manage the complete supply stream. Here you are looking for the "best suppliers" in total process management, best total cost, best innovation in process simplification, best consistent quality, and most creative turnkey customer solutions. In these examples, the market and benchmarking studies are aimed at finding the lowest total cost from suppliers as part of the initial screen. The objective is to seek the supplier that can provide lowest total cost and the simplest access and usage process.

A large midwestern financial services company was spending over $3 million annually for office supplies and desktop computer supplies at its headquarters location. It was sourcing office supplies through one supplier and using another for computer supplies. The supply arrangement was further complicated by a myriad of providers that sourced hundreds of the company's small offices across the country. The company was spending another $2 million for cut sheet paper and still another $4 million for computer paper. Every supplier involved was delivering and invoicing. Usage and inventory processes for office supplies were different from those for computer supplies. No information was collected or tracked to understand usage patterns, quality, or customer satisfaction.

The company conducted a comprehensive market study to develop its options for consolidating suppliers and was stunned at the level of process innovation available for something as simple as office and computer supplies.

The company turned to a leading-edge provider that offers a turnkey solution to managing the entire range of products to meet office and computer support needs. Its key innovation is single-source supply of all product needs at all company locations and direct delivery to the desk of the person ordering. In one broad stroke, it replaced thousands of individual, fragmented purchase transactions with a single standardized catalog of options that meet internal user needs. In so doing, it eliminates all on-site inventories, provides a single centralized information source of purchase and usage measurements, improves customer satisfaction, and eliminates non-value-adding time spent in customer shopping and ordering. This comprehensive supply arrangement permits electronic invoicing and payment, thus eliminating countless thousands of manual transactions.

In addition to all of these benefits, the new provider can consolidate total purchases for sheet paper and computer paper with one manufacturer and further improve costs by standardizing paper usage.

The annual benefit to the company for this strategy was $1.75 million in purchase savings, plus simpler deliveries and logistics, usage reporting, measurement, and program management. Anti-inflation targets and continual improvement goals were set. These goals ranged up to 7 percent for the typical three-year agreements, netting significant benefit to the acquiring company.

This case is a prime example of a turnkey supply management strategy from a "best" supplier.

The key strategy for non-core/standard materials and services is to aggressively seek out comprehensive total supply-stream strategies from suppliers who are process innovators.

Strategies for Core/Standard Materials and Services

Core/standard materials and services include a wide range of items from merchandising devices to consultants, basic chemicals and pigments, component parts, process equipment, and professional services.

Consulting purchases are high-expense areas within this category and include specific services such as marketing consulting, market research, product design, package design, advertising, public relations, and communications. These purchases tend to draw upon standard competencies and skills to meet unique and specific needs. Yet strategies can be applied to these purchases to guide consistent market selection and usage management in the same way as with more tangible purchases. In this case, however, the total cost benefits will derive from the standardization in a supplier selection and the actual process of planning and completing the work.

In this case supply leaders will complete market and benchmarking studies to seek out the "best" competencies and best-usage practices and create a structured process for describing deliverables and usage methods. Best practices for this category often link consultant compensation directly to the attainment of measurable goals.

The key to creating strategies for this group is to focus on the leading-edge suppliers and usage practices for any given purchase. In this way you are ensured of being able to create a specific strategy incorporating the very latest products, services, and usage practices. The supply strategy will emerge from engaging the supplier in managing portions of the supply stream and drawing upon its best practice knowledge to craft usage and access processes that will provide the lowest total cost.

Supply Strategy Classification and Development Guide Summary

Supply chain strategies are developed to maximize the value of purchase investments. This requires matching the best supplier capability with the purchase requirement *and* implementing the best strategy for lowest total cost at all relevant business locations.

The Classification Guide is a leadership tool to determine the supply strategy needs *before* accessing the marketplace. It is a good reference tool to help supply teams assure they are accessing the right balance of skills as they engage suppliers and develop plans to optimize supply streams. Most important, this guide will help you to create the right strategy to optimize total cost, without spending more than you need to spend for all-too-elegant solutions you don't need. It's easy to access the leading-edge features and processes for every purchase; that's not what supply chain optimization is about.

Reengineering Concepts and Tools for the Acquisition Process

Another aspect of the supply-stream strategy development falls outside the supply-stream matrix of Figure 7-1 but is equally important. This is the opportunity to eliminate all the non-value-adding work steps at the beginning of a new supplier relationship, thus freeing your supply leader to focus on continual improvement work.

Supplier consolidation provides the perfect opportunity to reengineer the acquisition and payable process. All too frequently old habits and procedures become entrenched and are automatically accepted without question as necessary. Often no routine mechanism exists to identify better methods and to systematically review processes as these supporting materials and services are purchased. Supply management provides that opportunity by requiring the supply management leader to understand the usage of goods and services purchased—not merely buy them. In any benchmarking or market analysis effort, therefore, better usage methods and systems are routinely surfaced for review by multifunctional users and leaders in order to evaluate better methods of purchase and use:

- Old procedures and tasks can be eliminated.
- New policies and procedures can be implemented.
- All non-value-adding steps can be removed.
- New measures and information tracking can be built into the new transactional process.

We have stressed the importance of value chain mapping the entire supply cycle from the inception of a need to be fulfilled all the way through receiving value at the end of the cycle. This will include all the repetitive transaction sections of the cycle. One of the high-frequency transaction areas to examine for reengineering is accounts payable.

Every type of transaction should be examined with the objective of eliminating it or automating it if elimination is impossible. You will find many new opportunities as your supplier base is consolidated and efforts shift to focus on real value. In all cases, you should eliminate non-value-adding transactions.

Figure 7-2 is a summary of acquisition and payment techniques that you should use to reengineer new purchase and payment methods with your consolidated supplier base. Information, banking, and credit technology are making new options available for supply managers to customize transactional flows and processes by material stream. This customization greatly increases a business's ability to manage these streams effectively.

Look carefully at Figure 7-2. These acquisition concepts and tools provide immediate reengineering opportunities with your consolidated supplier relationships. Think of these tools as part of a strategy to optimize the complete supply stream, not just as means to streamline transactional work.

Figure 7-2. Purchase and payment methods.

Purchase Cost		Low-Frequency Transaction	High-Frequency Transaction
	High Unit Cost	■ Contract payments ■ Request for quote ■ Purchase order ■ Evaluated receipt settlement (e.g., capital, consultants)	■ Pay on consumption ■ ERS (Evaluated Receipt Settlement) ■ Contracting blanket ■ EDI (Electronic Data Interchange) ■ Electronic commerce (Internet/intranet) ■ Consolidation ■ Alliances (e.g., core key material stream)
	Low Unit Cost	■ Purchasing card ■ Direct pay (e.g., miscellaneous supplies)	■ Purchase card ■ Evaluated Receipt Settlement ■ Electronic Data Interchange ■ Electronic commerce (Internet/intranet) ■ Consolidation ■ Consignment ■ Cost plus contract (e.g., distributors, MRO [maintenance, repairable and operating supplies])

Low-
Frequency
Transaction

High-
Freqency
Transaction

Transaction Frequency

Transactions of low frequency and low unit cost involve materials or services that are delivered all at once or at least in limited increments. In these instances the purchaser is looking for convenience and simplicity in the procurement process. Purchasing supply-stream–specific cards may be the best alternative for hardware store purchases if you have a small business or are at a small site. They're also ideal for a wide array of low-value or high-value transactions including refreshments and purchases for gatherings, for flowers, and for miscellaneous supplies. Replace petty cash, site drafts, and purchase orders. Simplify your life.

If you're dealing with transactions of low frequency and high cost, such as capital equipment, consider what you really want or need from the equipment and your supplier. Avoid the knee-jerk reaction of agreeing to a purchase template based on what you've always done or what the terms of the manufacturer happen to be. What's the problem you're trying to solve? When do you get value from the equipment? Can you pay when it starts to work effectively? Better still, can you pay when your customer actually uses the feature this equipment or software provides? Ask for alternatives in the request for quotation (RFQ) beyond what is specified. There may be payment options worth considering in addition to those you requested.

Use your purchase order not just to buy but to define your requirements fully and carefully. For expensive, one-time buys, you can't rely on resolving problems after the transaction is complete. Remember, by the time you dig out your contract to check the remediation clause, the damage has already occurred.

High-frequency transactions present the greatest opportunity for streamlining. High-frequency transactions that are low in unit cost typically involve all kinds of supplies. You want the convenience of easy purchase and summary information to manage overall usage.

Pay on receipt, known in accounting terms as evaluated receipt settlement (ERS), a new accounts payable procedure, is commonly used for repetitive items, eliminating the invoicing step and saving expense dollars for you and the supplier.

Electronic data interchange (EDI) is ideal for high-cost raw materials and supplies with a high volume of repetitive transactions, including purchase orders, invoices, shipping notices, and so on. Office products and other supplies can also be handled with automatic replenishment mechanisms or user-released electronic transmittal directly to the suppliers. These mechanisms create electronic summary invoicing and automatic payment within predetermined parameters. Electronic commerce via the Internet offers many of the same possibilities and is emerging as a flexible, low-cost option. Consolidation efforts for high-volume transactions is a priority area for any beginning supplier consolidation effort.

Think of working with suppliers that can provide genuine help from the beginning of the supply management process to its end. With your suppliers, rethink, remap, and reengineer your process and your supplier's at the same time.

IMPLEMENTATION GUIDE

This chapter has focused on developing and implementing supply management strategies. The prerequisite classification work will help you determine how to ensure that supplier resources are brought to bear on your supply operations, R&D, and support functions. This may mean outsourcing segments of your business if the expertise or efficiency of your suppliers warrants or if these segments are not part of your core competencies. This, in turn, determines the role you wish these purchases to play in your business. We have dealt, at some length, with how to do it, but you and other executive leaders must make these choices and set the direction.

Successfully implementing change requires understanding human nature. People are often threatened by change. By determining the supply strategy you and your supply management team believe is correct, you can implement change in a confident, integrated fashion and keep all the functional and business management segments in step all along the way.

At the other end of the spectrum, people willing to change naturally want to drive projects to the highest level of innovation. Software engineers and mechanical engineers, as well as operations support leaders, often attempt elegant solutions that reach for the state of the art. For certain purchase categories, these are correct solutions and the cost and resources expended are worth it in returned margins and market share. But for other purchases these are not the best solutions. The best solution may require the lowest cost or the fastest delivery. The way you categorize your requirements will help shape your outcome.

It falls to executive management to see that supply management strategies for the various supply streams are integrated in a way that ensures that they all contribute to your competitive advantage. This is not a task for the supply teams alone. They are not always coordinated and do not always make certain that benefits are returned in better cost, better service, improved functionality, or improved sales. Your close attention to these supply management strategies and their integration into your overall business strategies in a tangible way demonstrates an understanding and priority that will permeate the organization, ensuring the coordination and integration of these principles into the fabric of the business.

Summary

The supply strategy requirements are pretty straightforward, but unless these are clear before your teams begin, you will not maximize your opportunities. So, you choose your course of action—with your leadership direction. This all begins by defining the role and desired supply strategy characteristics for the purchases that support your business.

CHAPTER 8

The Supply Management Organization

The supply management organization is not a traditional pyramid structure for a new functional initiative that will replace the procurement organization. In fact, it isn't a structure at all. Rather, it is a comprehensive collection of *work tasks and role definitions, processes, organizational mechanisms,* and *competencies* that work together to span functional groupings and geographic and business locations.

How many times have you been party to the debates of centralization versus decentralization? The age-old listing of advantages and disadvantages always brings us to the quandary of how to provide strong, singular-focused leadership for a new initiative while making provision for various implementation tactics necessary to support different businesses and locations. Having lived through a number of these "corporate" change initiatives, which in itself should speak for something, we have heard the litany of complaints from the community of users (operating and business employees who are being asked to change their behavior in some way). These all served to help us understand why the uniqueness of these individuals and their respective organizations precluded participation in any effort requring change.

We heard time and time again:

"Our business is different."

"Our plant is different."

"Our product is different."

"Our service is special and different."

My shift is different; my equipment is different; my city, town, and state are different; my process is one of a kind; my customers are different (which is the only valid input to incorporate); and, finally, I'm different and my boss is *really* different.

In today's workplace, centralized organizational structures offering "one size fits all" solutions are being replaced by "seamless" structures—methods of focusing a cooperative blending of competencies on a specific business purpose. Rather than focusing on structures and organization charts, the new approach seeks to define the work and simply put in place those things necessary to complete it, share learning, and improve results over time. In this way business can create a new order of things without creating new structures and new overhead costs.

Supply Management Work Tasks and Roles

In carrying out the work of supply management—developing and implementing supply-stream strategies that maximize the value of expenditures for purchased materials and services—the supply leader has the following tasks:

- Conducting market/industry analysis
- Performing cost analysis
- Value chain mapping supply streams
- Defining total cost of ownership
- Benchmarking new methods and practices
- Developing continual improvement plans
- Reengineering material and transactional change
- Engaging users to change usage and access methods
- Measuring performance
- Managing supplier recources
- Providing supplier feedback
- Building individual supply management skills

These tasks are designed to deliver three types of outputs:

1. Analyses used to create supply strategies and plans for implementing improvements
2. Implementation of supply-stream strategies suggested in number 1
3. Measurement and learning to provide feedback and improve results

There are two different supply leader roles:

1. *The supply-stream leader* is accountable for optimizing the total supply stream by *developing* and implementing supply-stream strategies and improvement plans.
2. *The location supply leader* is accountable for optimizing a location's total purchase expenditure by *implementing* a number of supply-stream strategies at that location (plant site, business unit).

In practice, the leaders in these two roles work together as part of a team to develop supply strategies and select preferred suppliers. Once the strategy is developed, both supply leaders in these roles shift their emphasis to improvement and implementation work.

For the supply-stream leader, this work is managing supplier resources to implement the supply-stream changes at all locations and benchmarking market and usage practices in order to continually improve the supply-stream strategy and introduce innovations.

For the location supply leader, this work is engaging relevant users and implementing the actual usage and flow changes at the point of use.

At the end of the year, the supply-stream leader is accountable for competitive levels of performance or better for the *supply stream* at each location. Specific competitive measures compare total cost and usage practices.

The location supply leader is accountable for *overall purchased material* and service effectiveness at a given *location*. Specific measurements of supply strategy performance track availability, usage, and total cost.

Figure 8-1 depicts the different supply leader roles and their inter-relationships in a *supply network*. The Supply Network allows interested parties from different locations, including different business segments, to participate in the development and implementation of supply-stream strategies. The supply-stream leader and location supply leader roles are ongoing functional roles, responsible for actual supply-stream results and successful implementation. The other participants bring expertise and knowledge from other business or functional areas to help develop strategies and plans for implementation. They are not responsible for the actual ongoing implementation and improvement.

Figure 8-1. The supply network.

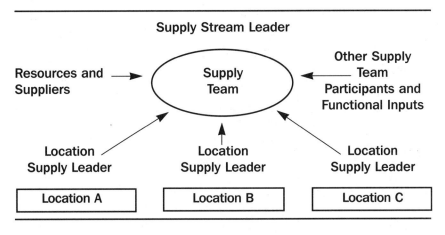

The supply network is like a cross-functional team except it crosses business units, locations, and often suppliers. In so doing it spans the barriers to implementation that often exist by ensuring that specific plans in fact deliver results directly beneficial to the specific point of use. The supply leader roles and the supply network are the building blocks of the supply management organization.

Supply Management Processes

As discussed in Chapter 5, the *consistent* use of the standard procurement, continual improvement, and innovation processes, shown in Table 8-1, will maximize the value of all purchase expenditures if applied to all supply streams. We think of these core processes as the supply leaders' guide to harnessing market potentials and creating and implementing supply-stream strategies.

Table 8-1. Major work steps in supply management core processes.

Procurement	Continual Improvement	Innovation
Define customer needs	Understanding customer usage	Defining customer requirements
Market analysis	Benchmarking usage and practices	Searching for sources of innovations
Supplier cost analysis	Creating options	Creating options
Supplier selection	Valuing and selecting options	Valuing options
Negotiation	Implementing continual improvement plans	Selection
Implementation and feedback	Measurement and learning	Implementation

Each process shares some common steps:

1. Begins with a customer focus.
2. Requires market-based analysis, creating fact-based options for improvement.
3. Develops specific implementation plans.

Each process begins with a customer analysis, which gives you the opportunity to take a fresh look at the purpose and required utility of the purchase. Business purchase streams are filled with products, services, and suppliers that someone selected based on intuitive judgment or because it met their personal needs. Most "overspecified" features in products stem from searching the marketplace for such "personal druthers." A customer focus, however, shifts the entire process to a factual platform, documenting levels of required functionality and usage patterns. This is the only way we know to separate the discretionary features from the essential requirements and link the purchase process to something for which the ultimate customer might be willing to pay.

The next step in each process is the market-based analysis. We believe this step is critical to tapping new ideas and avoiding the age-old lament, "We tried that before." The very nature of the market (and cost) analysis tasks creates improvement options based on facts: cost savings, new revenue, margin improvements, documented values, and so on. This work is important to create the rationale for changing suppliers or changing usage patterns. If users refuse such change in the face of this compelling logic, then some other agenda is working and it's time for someone to intervene.

Finally, each process guides the supply leader to a logical implementation plan, not another analysis or strategy that sits on a shelf. The implementation plans are comprehensive, including plans to involve all relevant participants affected by the change.

These core processes are used to source and rethink the sum total of all purchases of materials and services. They provide a standard approach for all supply streams and help the supply leaders seek out best appropriate market solutions to meet specified requirements.

Tables 8-2, 8-3, and 8-4 are process guideline checklists for each of the core processes. Each guideline describes the necessary key work within each of the major process steps, the concepts necessary to complete the work, and the outputs and results of each step. The work steps that are defined are the "value adding" supply management work.

New Supply Management Competencies

The supply leader seeks out market opportunities and practices as sources of new improvement for supply streams and is accountable for implementing change. In many ways the new sourcing role is like that of an internal product manager, requiring strong market and cost analytical skills and a broad understanding of all business functions. The role is often that of "enabler" of change—engaging relevant participants in the actual design of implementation plans and directing other resources to actually complete the work.

The majority of procurement personnel demonstrate the capability to acquire and practice new skills to perform this new work. Such skill building is critical to building new competencies and shifting participants from "reactive" buyers to "proactive" supply leaders. Skill requirements for the supply leader role fall into three categories:

1. New functional skills in supply management or market or cost analysis
2. Team dynamics and interpersonal skills
3. Leadership and project-planning skills

Tables 8-5, 8-6, and 8-7 illustrate the functional skill requirements for each major step. These skills can be acquired more rapidly and be readily reinforced if supply leaders are provided supporting learning aids and tools. Examples of these are also included in these illustrations.

The new functional skills are best developed through a curriculum that systematically helps participants apply the concepts in active workshop settings.

(text continues on page 156)

Table 8-2. Procurement process guidelines.

The market and supplier evaluation process to determine "best suppliers" to meet a material/service need. Results in consolidating the supply base.

Major Process Steps

Define Customer Needs	Market Analysis	Supplier Cost Analysis	Supplier Selection	Negotiation	Implementation and Feedback
■ Engage internal customers to identify: Core requirements Benefits Features	■ Develop market analysis, including: Competitor suppliers Buyers Suppliers New contracts Substitutes Trends	■ Define cost structure for the low-cost producer	■ Delineate selection criteria	■ Define final proposal requirements: Resource requirements Specific improvement goals Measurements Cash cost goals	■ Define location specific plans to transition current usage to new preferred suppliers

(continues)

Table 8-2. (*continued*)

	Major Process Steps				
Define Customer Needs	Market Analysis	Supplier Cost Analysis	Supplier Selection	Negotiation	Implementation and Feedback
■ Refine end market for sourcing	■ Define/identify: Low-cost products Distinctive market leader	■ Define cost structures for candidate suppliers	■ Develop short list of potential suppliers	■ Entertain final proposal submissions	■ Define communications plan
	■ Engage suppliers to present their business and market strategies plus a complete capabilities review	■ Define average industry Profit margin Variable cost Fixed cost		■ Complete supplier analysis	■ Define performance measures and schedule periodic reviews
					■ Schedule performance feedbacksessions
					■ Ongoing relation management toassure results

Major Concepts Required for Each Step

■ Customer and product definition	■ Market analysis	■ Supplier cost analysis	■ Criteria matrices	■ Business/project plan development
■ Refining the delivery system	■ Supplier strategy analysis and life cycle			

Outputs and Results of Each Step

■ Defines the industry to be sourced	■ Defines suppliers (to determine those with the most competitive advantage)	■ Defines industry cost structure	■ Preliminary supplier proposals	■ Specific proposals	■ Definitive consolidation plan for relevant business units/locations
■ Defines core technical requirements, features, and benefits	■ Defines industry structure and points of leverage	■ Supplier variable and fixed cost	■ Opportunities for leverage and improvement	■ Defines improvement goals and resource commitments	■ Resources, goals, timing, and measures
	■ Defines supplies strategies	■ Technical evaluation of suppliers			

The complete supply team is encouraged to participate in the capability-building workshops. In this way, they not only increase the value of their contribution but also become informed leaders of change as they return to their functional organizations. Since the procurement process by definition begins the reevaluation and consolidation of suppliers, the participants are limited to internal cross-business members. However, as the supply team gets ready to begin optimizing the supply stream, it is essential to include supplier resources who will help to design and implement improvements. Similarly, the suppliers' resources remain involved during the innovation search so as to prepare for technology and cost shifts that will affect the supply stream.

The capability-building plan creates a forum for supply teams to apply concepts, share learning from different supply streams, and reinforce the concept benefits. The intangible benefits accrue from building an expanded network of competent new supply leaders, who can call upon one another as sounding boards and sources of solutions to overcome implementation snags.

Benchmarking among organizational development experts indicates that best competencies within organizations are developed through a minimum of ninety hours of functional skill building every year. Moreover, the accountability to self-develop these skills is actually a part of the individual's annual goals.

The curriculum described in Table 8-8 meets this level of learning emphasis. In subsequent years of training, you would retain this workshop and supply team format but shift course content to building supply-stream strategies and more complex problem solving.

(text continues on page 166)

Table 8-3. Continual improvement process guidelines.

The planning process to identify opportunities for optimizing material/service flow and usage, and directing suppliers' resources to implement continual improvement plans. Results in reduced total cost of ownership and eliminating non-value-adding work.

		Major Process Steps			
Understanding Customer Usage	Benchmarking Usage and Best Practices	Creating Options	Value and Selecting Option	Implementing Continual Improvement Plan	Feedback and Learning
■ Value chain mapping of current material/service flows, including: Actual usage process All transactional steps	■ Benchmark relevant industry for best usage practices Collect specific usage benchmark measures Identify material/ service delivery processes to reduce cycle time Identify trans-actional processes to eliminate non-value-adding work steps	■ Engage customer and supplier resources to share benchmarking and "should cost" analysis	■ Engage customer and supplier resources to size the value and difficulty of improvement options	■ Develop time sequence for implementation	■ Engage suppliers and customers in periodic review of performance vs. measures

(continues)

Table 8-3. (continued)

| | Major Process Steps (continued) | | | | |
Understanding Customer Usage	Benchmarking Usage and Best Practices	Creating Options	Value and Selecting Option	Implementing Continual Improvement Plan	Feedback and Learning
■ Develop total cost of ownership (current) understanding	■ Develop "should cost" model for material/service	■ Engage customer and supplier resources to develop relevant opportunities for improvement	■ Prioritize options for implementation	■ Engage supplier resources to develop implementation plan	■ Develop plan to correct course or accelerate improvement implementation
■ Engage customer and supplier to evaluate and develop usage measures (how to measure effectiveness)			■ Build new total cost of ownership model with improvements in place	■ Develop internal and supplier communication plan for change	■ Recycle
				■ Create measures of performance	

Major Concepts Required for Each Step

■ Value chain mapping (value-adding, essential, and non-value-adding work identification) ■ Total cost of ownership	■ Transactional tools for streamlining work processes ■ "Should cost" mapping	■ Scoping opportunities	■ Prioritizing methodology	■ Business/project plan development	■ Building supply stream measures

Output and Results of Each Step

■ Definition of the current material/service process ■ Current total cost of ownership ■ Areas of improvement	■ Specific usage benchmarks ■ New process, practice, opportunities	■ Definitive improvement opportunities with tangible values	■ Ranking and prioritization of options based on opportunity and difficulty of implementation	■ Definitive continual improvement plan with goals, measures, resources, and timing	■ Learning and upgrading the plan

Table 8-4. Innovation process guidelines.

The innovation search for significant change in technology or process that can dramatically improve competitive advantage of the supply stream.

		Major Process Steps			
Defining Customer Requirements	*Searching for Sources of Innovation*	*Creating Options*	*Value Options*	*Selection*	*Implementation*
■ Engage internal customers to restate core requirements and prioritized benefits	■ Conduct market search for innovation leaders	■ Engage customer to review satisfaction analysis and market search	■ Engage customer teams to characterize innovative options	■ Engage customer and business leadership to review options and benefits	■ Develop innovation plan
■ Complete satisfaction of requirements analysis	■ Evaluate innovation in alternative technologies	■ Develop time-elapsed view of current value chosen for material/service flow	■ Sort options by magnitude of impact and level of competition advantage	■ Select path forward	■ Create prototype team
■ Define innovation readiness	■ Evaluate time-based opportunities for cycle time change	■ Engage customer and supplier resources in innovation prototyping session			■ Establish periodic review schedule to provide for feedback and learning

Major Concepts Required for Each Step

- Definition of core requirements and prioritization of benefits
- Life cycle analysis
- Time-based competition
- Market modeling for new entrants and substitutes
- "Benchmarking" for innovation
- Innovation prototyping
- Scoping options
- Business/project capital plan development

Outputs and Results of Each Step

- Satisfaction level analysis and readiness for innovation
- Definition of alternative technologies, applications and processes that deliver same/similar benefits
- New combinations of technologies that create new processes, usage, or delivery systems
- Definition and scoping of changes and impacts
- Prioritization of opportunities
- Business project plan to define and lead major change

Table 8-5. The procurement process skills.

To consolidate material and service purchase with "best suppliers."

Major Steps	Key Concepts	Tools	Skill Requirements
Defining the customer need and product definition	■ Customer and product definition ■ Refining the delivery system	■ Guidelines for defining core need, benefits, features (including technical specifications)	■ Interpersonal relationship understanding
Market analysis	■ Market analysis (Porter model) ■ Supplier strategy analysis ■ Life cycle analysis	■ Supplier request for business and market strategies ■ Porter model ■ Supplier evaluation model (factor sorting) ■ Market analysis format	■ Market analysis
Supplier value and cost analysis	■ Supplier cost analysis	■ Supply leader guidelines ■ "Should cost" model development	■ Financial statement understanding ■ Cost modeling
Supplier selections	■ Criteria matrices	■ Define final proposal requirements ■ Risk/legal analysis criteria	
Negotiation			
Implementation	■ Business/project plan development	■ Business/project plan plus format and guidelines	■ Defining requirements ■ Project planning ■ Supplier relationships ■ Communications

Table 8-6. The continual improvement process skills.

To optimize the total cost of ownership for the supply stream utilizing best supplier practices and resources.

Major Steps	Key Concepts	Tools	Skill Requirements
■ Defining customer usage	■ Value chain mapping ■ Total cost of ownership ■ "Should cost" modeling	■ Guide to value chain mapping ■ Total cost of ownership formula and process ■ "Should cost" modeling and design ■ How to understand usage effectiveness	■ Value chain mapping ■ Building representative cost models ■ Defining measures and necessary data collection
■ Search for best usage process practice ■ Creating options	■ Transactional tools for streamlining work processes ■ Scoping opportunities	■ User's guide to search for best practices and benchmarking ■ Option formats	■ Communications and interview skills ■ Facilitating and brainstorming
■ Valuing and selecting options	■ Prioritizing methodology	■ Qualifying benefits and outcomes ■ Prioritization of dollar impact and degree of difficulty	■ Sorting options and factor analysis
■ Implementing a continual improvement plan ■ Feedback and learning	■ Business plan/project plan development ■ Building supply-stream measures	■ Planning guide to sequence/state improvement changes ■ Usage measurements	■ Project planning ■ Communications ■ Supply management measurements

Table 8-7. The innovation process skills.

To search for a significant change in technology or process that dramatically improves supply stream competencies advantage.

Major Steps	Key Concepts	Tools	Skill Requirements
■ Defining customer requirements	■ Prioritization of customer benefits ■ Life cycle analysis ■ Satisfaction analysis	■ Guide for innovation readiness (questions and life cycle analysis)	■ Intro to time-based competition ■ Life cycle analysis
■ Searching for sources of innovation	■ Time base completion ■ Market modeling for new entrants and substitutes ■ Benchmarking for innovation	■ Guide to innovation "benchmarking"	■ Innovation benchmarking techniques
■ Creating options	■ Innovation prototyping	■ Brainstorming guide	■ Enabling prototyping sessions
■ Valuing and selecting options	■ Scoping options	■ Quantifying benefits and outcomes ■ Prioritization of opportunities	■ Modeling opportunities and sizing impacts ■ Sorting options
■ Implementation of major change		■ Project/capital improvement plan guide	■ Project planning ■ Communications

Table 8-8. Typical curriculum for core processes learning.

Procurement Process	Continual Improvement	Innovation
Intro to Supply Management	Intro to Continual Improvement	Intro to Innovation
Market Industry Analysis	Value Chain Mapping	Time-Based Competition
Suppliers' Business Strategies	Total Cost of Ownership	Satisfaction of Requirements and Readiness for Innovation Analysis
Life Cycle Analysis	Cycle Time Analysis	Search for Innovation
Intro to Value Chain Mapping	Benchmarking	Innovation Prototyping
Building a Supplier Consolidation Plan	"Should Cost" Modeling	Building the Innovation Plan
Implementing and Engaging Supplies	Creating and Valuing Options	
	Developing Continual Improvement Plan	
<u>Class Time:</u> 2–5 days	2–5 days	2–3 days
<u>Work Time:</u> 6–10 weeks	4–6 weeks	4–6 weeks

This competency training becomes a functioning part of the supply management organization, and is key not only to building skill but also enhancing cross-organizational problem solving and change. In addition to these functional skills, supply team members can simultaneously participate in general business effectiveness skill building within their respective business areas. Opportunities abound to enhance skills in project planning, time management, leadership, team effectiveness, and on and on.

The new currency in organizational effectiveness is the individual's ability to scale barriers and help create mechanisms for change. Corporate survivors are ever mindful of acquiring techniques to build these skills. We expect this base of skill to develop broadly across the organization as a whole, independent of any supply management initiative. The new dimension here is simply a new functional skill set that must be put in place.

Experience has demonstrated that it requires one and a half to two years to "reskill" a procurement workforce to achieve competent levels of supply management work. Within this time period, actual benefits are received and momentum increases. Truly brilliant supply-stream models of change will emerge and motivate others to participate. By the third full year supply leadership candidates will proliferate.

Finally, these are new, finite, tangible skills to be developed. This is not a transformation of mortals to superhumans, rather a skill-level increase from buyer to supply leader. The ability to create a new corporate competence in supply management is eminently doable within two to three years.

Like most things worth having, it takes some effort and lots of leadership.

New Supply Management Mechanisms

Supply leaders armed with a full complement of supply management skills are capable of crafting and implementing the supply-stream strategies. They do, however, require broad organizational support to build awareness and agreement to adopt new procurement and purchase usage behavior. This support must provide four key elements:

1. Broad organizational communications
2. Conflict resolution and barrier removal
3. Setting priorities
4. Determining common measures and rewards

As the early supply teams begin to multiply their efforts, supply management work accelerates on many different supply streams simultaneously. Because the very nature of the work spans organizational boundaries, the teams are met with varied degrees of acceptance and cooperation. Frankly the normative reception is more in line with, "You're with Procurement? And you want to do what? Sorry!"

Good supply leaders and teams will arm themselves with communications material and strong logic and eventually convince most audiences to value the promised benefits. This process, however, can take inordinately long, further delaying the benefits of purchase leverage savings and usage improvements.

The most important feature of the supply management work is that the benefits accrue at implementation. Invoice savings, usage and time savings, and reduced processing costs all occur *after* supplier consolidation and new purchase usage patterns are in place. Building organizational support is not just a nice cultural add-on to the project's effectiveness; it is imperative to accelerate the supply management implementation phase and collect the benefits in the form of P&L savings.

Building organizational receptivity begins with creating broad awareness of the goals and concepts. While the executive leaders may have sent the early messages, the organization will need many reinforcing messages in order to set the stage for real acceptance and change. These communications are best received from key business and functional leaders who demonstrate their desire to integrate supply management practices into their business priorities. The actual form of the communications can vary from presentations, videos, staff meetings, memos, brown bag lunch forums, formal addresses, and managing by walking around—any communication, repeated again and again so that participants become willing conspirators in seeking new benefits.

The communications efforts will go a long way to creating an environment conducive to change. However, issues of conflict and priority for the implementation work will require organizational intervention for resolution. Implementing a supply management process is all-important to the supply leaders and of little importance to everyone else. Even after "seeing the light" of the compelling logic and benefits, participants will agree with a resounding "Yes, but later!" Rather than deal with these situations as they arise and move through the predictable agony of watching opposing sides surface the issues through layers of organizational structure, the successful implementers anticipate problems with organizational mechanisms.

There are three types of mechanisms that are helpful in this implementation process: leadership mechanisms, integrating mechanisms, and functional mechanisms.

Leadership Mechanisms

These mechanisms are cross-functional and cross-business executive-level groups that assemble for the purpose of supporting the supply management goals. Their work as a group addresses communications, sets organizational priorities for implementation, resolves conflict, removes barriers, defines tangible measures of success, and provides rewards for success. These groups are generally facilitated by the supply management head, who brings the planning context, schedules, conflicts, and results to the forum session. The group works together to solve the agenda items and acts individually within the respective business groups to communicate direction and priorities.

BASF North America, a large chemicals producer, has been implementing the supply management process for one and a half years. The company began the work with early pilot efforts on supply streams to prove the validity of supply team ideas and achieve tangible results. With results in hand, the supply leaders engaged the executive committee, which acted as the main sponsor for the roll-out of the supply management process. The committee set the objectives for savings goals and timing. Key to success, however, was the way in which the committee members created organizational mechanisms to deal with priorities and conflict. Figure 8-2 depicts the BASF supply management organizational structure.

In the BASF model, each organizational mechanism has a clearly defined role and its own work:

Executive sponsors (composed of three executive vice-presidents)	■ Set direction, goals, and timing. ■ Review results. ■ Recognize achievement.

Figure 8-2. BASF supply management organizational structure.

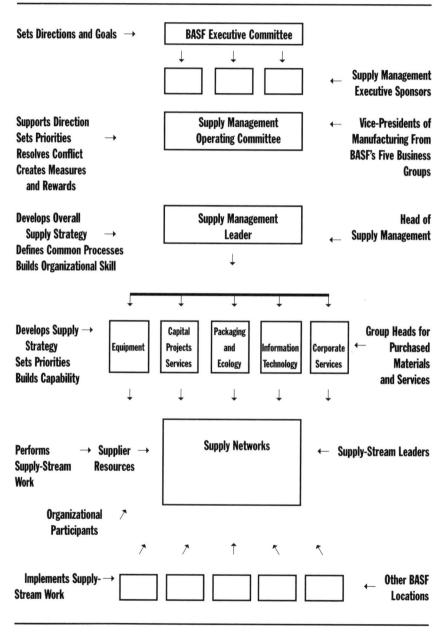

Operating counsel (Composed of five vice-presidents of manufacturing from BASF five business groups)	■ Reinforce direction. ■ Set priorities. ■ Resolve conflict. ■ Establish measures of success and rewards.
The supply management head	■ Develops the overall supply management strategy. ■ Defines common processes and policies. ■ Builds organization capability.
The group purchasing leaders	■ Provide direction to aggregate of supply-stream networks. ■ Build capability. ■ Set implementation priority.
Supply network	■ Creates and implements supply-stream strategies.
Supply leaders	■ Implement supply strategies. ■ Measure results.

The mechanisms created in this example are "leadership mechanisms." They all work to set direction and clear the way for successful implementation. With this simple group structure, BASF has found a way to span five totally distinctive major business groups with a common business process. The process happens to be led by a corporate supply management head, with a staff of supply leaders. The bulk of the implementation, however, happens at the various business and manufacturing locations. This work is led by those local supply leaders.

A second example of leadership mechanisms is the creation of a sourcing council, which consists of relevant functional or business leaders more directly related to the purchased material or service outcomes. For example, a sourcing council might be created to oversee all information technology related purchases, including all hardware, software, and professional and contracted services. In large service businesses, such as banks and telecommunications companies, annual purchases of these materials and services can exceed $500 million per year.

In this case, the sourcing council would consist of the chief information officer, the supply management head, the service or systems technology head, and the comptroller. These executives together are best prepared to set priorities for supply-stream work because they most closely relate to the technical priorities in the information technology area. In this example, the council might actually review specific supply-stream strategies and value and approve continual improvement work. Such councils can be created for major groupings of related purchased materials and services. In the BASF example, an actual organization role—that of group supply leader—replaces these councils by providing this strategic direction.

The supply management head in your business would have the best sense of where strategy issues and priority issues arise and require resolution and direction.

Integrating Mechanisms

An integrating mechanism can be something as simple as incorporating supply management as a regular item on staff meeting agendas in major functional and business reviews. The purpose is to keep the supply management goals, progress, and other issues before the relevant organizational leaders. For years, procurement, as a lower-level administrative function, has reported to plant comptrollers or administrative service leaders—all clearly out of the mainstream of the business value chain. The essence of the supply management process value derives from increasing your organizational contact with the marketplace to integrate new usage and improvement practices for your business. An administrative leader cannot provide the access or direction necessary for success. So, rather than getting into another reorganizational tizzy about where to report, use organizational mechanisms to engage the relevant leaders who will benefit from these process results. We think of integrating mechanisms as periodic opportunities to "integrate" the supply management process, issues, and future steps into the business fabric.

In this way supply management, like human resources or budgeting, becomes a periodic agenda item for review and priority discussion. These reviews become an excellent opportunity to measure results, share learning, set new priorities, resolve differences, and change course where necessary. In our experience the local supply leaders and supply-stream leaders are the best equipped to resource these periodic reviews with up-to-date information on supply-stream and location implementation progress.

Functional Mechanisms

While the supply management organization we describe is a pretty flat, broad, free-form collection of supply networks and supply leaders, it does require its own leadership to ensure that implementation work is successfully completed and learning is shared. We see two types of functional mechanisms directly aimed at these objectives.

The *capability-building* workshops quickly become the learning forum. In addition to meeting periodically for gaining hands-on workshop skills, these groups begin to share implementation techniques, ways to measure success, and methods to engage their relevant business leaders.

Many organizations create "classes" of participants who progress through several skill-building workshops together so that these cross-networking relationships can be developed. Class I might consist of five to six teams, all focused on various equipment purchases, with participants from all locations. Class II might consist of another six teams, all involved in administration support purchase from corporate and headquarters locations. After sharing three workshop sessions to learn the three core processes over the course of one year, these "classes" become an informal network in themselves for sharing tips and real learning.

We encourage organizations beginning to implement a supply management process to create this "learning" mechanism as part of its skill-building program. While we cannot directly measure its impact, we continually see first-hand the benefits to implementation success. In an inspiring way, these groups become a jury of peers who set their own standards for performance and motivate better and better successes.

The *supply management leadership* forum is the second functional mechanism. This group is composed of the major supply-stream leaders and the major location supply leaders and is responsible for integrating the supply-stream and location objectives and priorities. Location supply leaders are faced with implementing change across many supply streams. Similarly, supply-stream leaders and the supply management head are charged with implementing change across all supply streams in order to optimize an organization's total cost of ownership. The leadership forum simply brings these two leadership perspectives together quarterly so that progress is shared, issues are raised, resources are directed, and new priorities are set.

The supply management head leads this group and ensures its effectiveness with relevant instruction, learning, benchmarking and outside resources where needed. Finally, the supply management head can take issues from this forum and elevate them to the other leadership groups as necessary.

The leadership, integrating, and functional mechanisms are flexible organizational tools that replace old organizational layers and formal roles.

The general formula for selecting mechanisms to create the appropriate supply management organization for your business is to decide which will work best for your specific culture and leadership capabilities. The Implementation Guide at the end of this chapter is designed to help you to answer these questions.

We are convinced that implementing organizations are "Just do it!" machines that are empowered to truly "have at it." This spirit comes from putting people and teams in an environment that motivates and recognizes their successes. The last thing these people and teams need is a lot of structure and layers. Having experienced firsthand the freedom of far-flung groups and teams held together by a thin fabric of council meetings and periodic reviews, we can only attest to the ever increasing energy level that directly translates to growing results.

IMPLEMENTATION GUIDE

Creating your own supply management organization in a nontraditional way can be the greatest signal that this business effort is different and real.

You will need a couple of pieces of knowledge to begin your planning. The first is a view of purchased spending by business type, by location, and ideally by product or service type (eg., equipment, chemicals, information technology). The second is a view of your current organizational structure by major business type and function.

Finally, it would be of immense help to have a supply management head in mind, so that you can work together to shape a new organizational map.

With this knowledge in hand, you should answer the following questions.

1. Which most senior executive leaders would make the best supply management sponsors? Pick no more than three. These are senior executives who understand and value the benefits, have some vision of the required change, and are prepared to confront policy and organization structure to give the new benefits.

2. How is your business structured? Highly centralized? Highly decentralized? Which are the most important key functions? Finance? R&D? Information technology? List the ten most "make it happen" leaders in your business. The list you have compiled will include business and functional leaders, who should use one or more leadership mechanisms to clear the path for successful implementation.

Where in the organization will the greatest change occur? Manufacturing? Key Functions? Key Businesses? Broadly across all locations and functions?

1. If the purchase expenditures are fairly broadly spent, a leadership steering or operating committee is the place to start. Do you need location heads as participants, or heads of major function types, e.g., manufacturing?

2. If the purchases are concentrated in big groups by business or function, a working council mechanism will be necessary to guide strategic direction and priorities. Is there more than one large grouping? If yes, then identify these groups.

- Decide which mechanism(s) is most appropriate for your organization.
- Decide who from your list should participate in each mechanism.
- Select names for these mechanisms:
  —Steering Committee?
  —Supply Management Operating Committee?
  —Purchase Councils?

3. Define the role of this (or these) mechanism. It should include:

- Reinforce direction, with goals and timing.
- Set priorities by purchase supply stream, business, and location.
- Develop organizational communications.
- Develop measures of success.
- Develop rewards and recognition programs.

4. Define how to integrate supply management goals into current organizational structures. Which integrating mechanisms may be most appropriate?

- Business staff meetings? How often?
- Functional staff meetings? How often?
- Executive staff meetings? How often?

What should agenda address?

- Progress to date?
- Key supply-stream strategies to be implemented?
- Descriptions of major changes?
- Priorities by business/location?
- Measures of success?
- Annual benefits forecast?

5. Define supply management functional organization.

- What are major groupings of purchased materials and services? (No more than six.)
- Do you have capable leaders for these supply groupings? With procurement? In related functions?
- How quickly can you create this organizational capability? 1 month? 3 months? 6 months?
- Identify the pilot supply networks. Identify actual supply streams and supply leaders.
- Develop a view of the supply leadership team. Name key supply-stream (or group supply) leaders Name key location leaders
- Evaluate supply leaders' capability with regard to supply management competencies. Leadership skills? Organizational skills?

- How will you build organizational skill? Curricula? Timing?

6. How can you best support companywide communications?

- Have supply management head create common set of communication tools, including presentations, videos, brochures.
- Ask steering committees to review the respective businesses and locations.
- Review with executive committee.
- Meet with all employees by video/mail.

Working through these six questions will give you a good draft of an implementation organization.

Summarize notes and meet with your peers and key subordinants to refine.

CHAPTER 9

Measuring Effectiveness

We have defined supply management as a methodology for examining all facets of the buying and actual use of purchased materials and services. We have indicated that many procurement departments are consolidating suppliers and implementing national, even global, agreements with those suppliers but are failing to create the strategies necessary to maximize their value and to minimize their total cost of ownership.

What are the reasons for this? Many don't fully understand the concept of supply management or have difficulties implementing the process even if they do. One of the most important success factors in implementing any project or process, once a clear understanding and definition are in place, is a way to measure effectiveness. What specifically are you trying to do? What are your own people expected to do and what are the suppliers expected to do to ensure maximization of value?

Regular and reliable measurements are important in any business activity. Businesses are continually balancing performance—including quality and time—with cost. This is not an easy task. Each must be carefully defined so that measurement is quantifiable. Then when cost goes up without corresponding increases in performance or value, or when performance or value slips without cost decreases, you know you have a problem. If either cost or performance is a specific competitive advantage for you, then even trade-offs are not acceptable. In any case, you need to measure.

Early work to define measures for these new supply concepts created awareness about the importance of total costs versus purchase costs, but little has been written about a set of measurements for this new managing process. At best, supply leaders intuitively apply their knowledge of total life cycle to specific material purchases. Specific measures that capture all component costs and usage variables remain widely unknown. Furthermore, until only recently no systematic measurement process was available to effectively understand and track the value maximization of purchased material/service streams.

In the fall of 1995, procurement periodicals were finally publicizing the "new supply management concepts" but widely proclaiming:

> *"Measurements for the new supply management concepts have yet to be created."*

We describe in this chapter the definitive performance measures for supply management, thus ending the mystery of how to maximize the value of dollars spent on sourced materials and services.

This approach is vastly different from the micro-accounting measures relied on from the 1950s until—sad to say—the present. Pricing history, standard cost dollars, and other effectiveness measures do not go far enough, and procurement efficiency measures such as budget per purchasing employee and procurement head count are ineffective in determining whether or not supply management benefits are being realized as they should be.

Measures are intended to be a learning tool to help an organization correct its course and improve performance. Increasingly, however, businesses are realizing that the measurements they choose actually drive the behavior of their employees and are not necessarily connected with the intended goals. In short, you become what you measure. The fact is, you can rarely collect the appropriate information to measure performance or progress, so you settle for the data you can collect. This often provides a tactical view of a situation with little learning about the sources of problems or new opportunities.

As discussed in Chapter 3, the traditional procurement process has become a transactional process aimed at finding and buying materials and services, getting them delivered to the internal user, and paying the supplier. Often these measurements even include "efficiency" indicators of the number of purchase orders per buyer over time, or cost per purchase order, which add little to the value you should derive from your procurement professionals and supply base.

Because the supply base is typically fragmented in large businesses, it's virtually impossible to track the myriad transactions that occur during one purchasing year. Even on-line purchasing systems that report all the direct and indirect purchases for an organization track only price paid and amounts used. Neither the price history nor the quantity history constitutes a "measurement" of the total effectiveness of the purchased material or service. As with many other business-tracking procedures, you get data rather than information:

Typical Procurement Measurements

- Pricing history
- On time/complete deliveries
- Units or hours purchased

So let's begin again by asking, What do I want to know about the effectiveness of the supply management process to be sure it's working? From a supply-stream viewpoint, what are the relevant indicators?

The entire measurement process is aimed at not only applying metrics to quantifiable usage data, but also providing indicators about the alignment of supplier values and resources with your own competitive requirements and values. Are your objectives and the supplier's objectives the same? You are looking for a way to get feedback to see how you're doing by using representational measures and supplementing them with subjective questioning: How can we improve? Have the supply-stream objectives been met? Are these still the right objectives to meet customer needs? Are we getting the products/services we expected?

There are only three main questions to answer regarding supply management effectiveness:

1. How effective is the material or service *supply-stream strategy* in maximizing value for your dollars spent?
2. How effective is the supply management *process* in implementing that strategy?
3. How effective is that strategy versus your *competitors'* strategy for the same material/service?

Let's examine these more closely.

Material/Service Supply-Stream Effectiveness

The effectiveness of a material or service stream is determined by understanding the cost and time components for the total stream of use. This includes all the acquisition costs plus actual usage costs, maintenance and training costs, environmental impact costs, and the time required to deliver the value from the purchase stream.

Clearly, a rather complex set of data is required to understand these many dimensions. So let's aggregate the data into some representational models, as shown in Table 9-1, so that we are able to develop a strategic view of the delivery stream's effectiveness. It is important that the measurements in Table 9-1 be viewed comprehensively. They are important as a total picture of what is happening,

Table 9-1. Supply stream effectiveness.

Specific Performance Models	Information for Tracking
Acquisition costs (e.g., price, terms, discounts, cost of inventory supplier selection, qualification, purchasing administration)	■ Invoice pricing with stipulated discount, terms.
Total cost of ownership $TCO = A + $ Present Value of $(O + T + M + W + E - S)*$	■ Total inventory value (storerooms, floor stock, supplier inventory, warehouse inventory)—going down? ■ Usage measures (e.g., waste, scrap, units present, efficiency, life cycle)—going down?
Cycle time ■ Total time from need to usage ■ Waiting time versus working time	■ Total time spent, waiting time, working time—to what data point? ■ Number of employees involved in supply work tasks.
"Should cost" analysis	■ Industry variable and fixed-cost research.

*A = acquisition cost, O = operating costs, T = training costs, M = maintenance, W = warehousing, E = environmental costs, S = salvage value.

as trends indicating how it's all coming together. The four measures shown are necessary to fully evaluate the effectiveness of a material or service stream:

Acquisition Costs

Acquisition costs measure how effectively you have sourced the marketplace. Cash costs indicate total acquisition costs, including inventory cost, and reveal chosen suppliers' ability to provide competitive costs. These costs, however, are usually only a relatively small percentage of the total cost of ownership—generally not more than 35 percent in the case of materials, never more than 90 percent for services.

Specific information that must be tracked to construct these measures includes invoiced pricing histories, specific discounts, rebates and other terms, plus actual inventory values in stock at all locations.

Total Cost of Ownership (TCO)

As discussed in detail in Chapter 5, TCO measures the effectiveness of the total strategy in procuring and managing the entire delivery stream. The total cost is a representational model of all facets of the delivery system (purchased materials stream).

TCO includes the acquisition costs plus actual usage effectiveness (scrap, waste, utility in process, etc.), necessary training prior to use, required maintenance to ensure continued use, and warehousing and environmental impact, if applicable. If at the end of the life cycle of the supply stream materials can be sold for reuse or salvage, these revenues are deducted from the total cost.

TCO analysis is essential to understanding the costs beyond price, which has been all too often relied upon as the primary measure of purchase value. To shift this emphasis, you may want to do as several companies have done and identify a person or team to maintain a focus on this bigger picture, ensuring that this element of total cost is not only correctly accounted for in supporting purchasing decisions but carried through into product costing and the other appropriate accounting systems across the business.

For the sake of simplicity, we have not identified the costs of quality as a separate element of TCO. Volumes have been written on that subject. For our purposes here, we have chosen to assume that costs of poor quality will be captured under operations cost.

Keki R. Bhote, in his 1989 *Strategic Supply Management,* used an excellent graphic (Figure 9-1) to identify both the visible and hidden costs of poor quality. Obviously, this is an enormous threat to the fortunes of any business; but it also affords great opportunity, because the supply management measurements serve to highlight these costs, along with the others, for continual improvement and proactive resolution.

Joseph M. Juran, the quality pioneer and a contemporary of Deming's, suggests seven points that a supply management leader can use to address quality issues. Numerous Deming and Juran writings are widely available.

Juran's Seven-Point Sequence for a Quality Breakthrough

1. Breakthrough in attitude, away from control and fire fighting.
2. Project identification, using the Pareto principle for identifying the vital few (20 percent or less) causes accounting for the largest portion (80 percent or more) of the economic impact.

Figure 9-1. The hidden costs of poor quality.

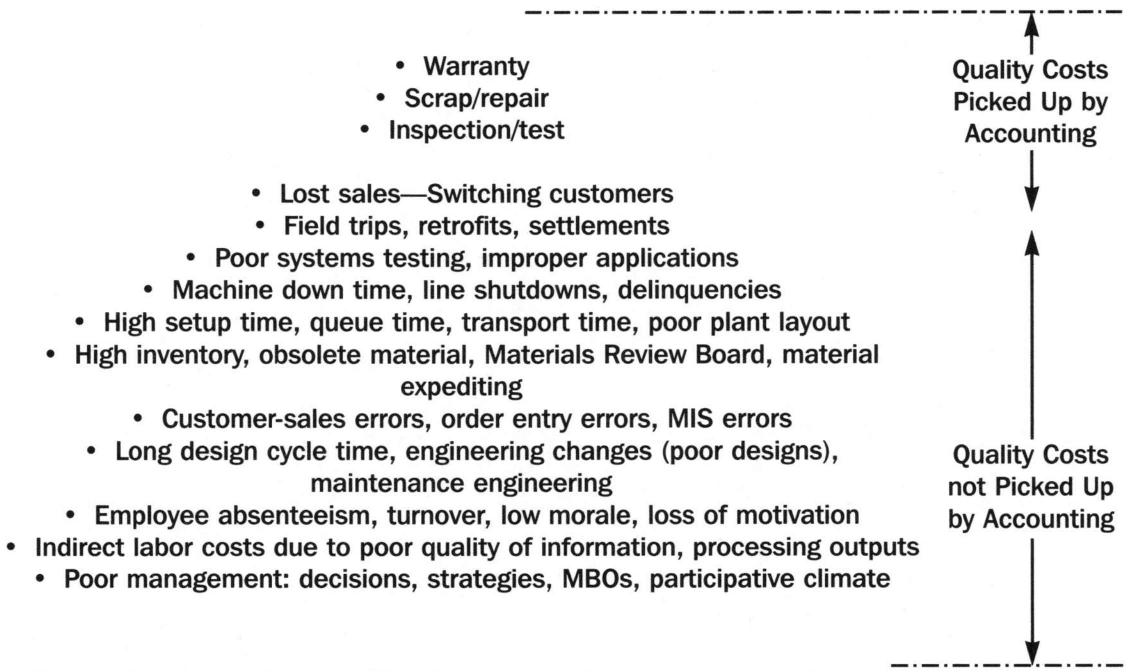

Quality Costs Picked Up by Accounting

- Warranty
- Scrap/repair
- Inspection/test

Quality Costs not Picked Up by Accounting

- Lost sales—Switching customers
- Field trips, retrofits, settlements
- Poor systems testing, improper applications
- Machine down time, line shutdowns, delinquencies
- High setup time, queue time, transport time, poor plant layout
- High inventory, obsolete material, Materials Review Board, material expediting
- Customer-sales errors, order entry errors, MIS errors
- Long design cycle time, engineering changes (poor designs), maintenance engineering
- Employee absenteeism, turnover, low morale, loss of motivation
- Indirect labor costs due to poor quality of information, processing outputs
- Poor management: decisions, strategies, MBOs, participative climate

From: Keki R. Bhote, *Strategic Supply Management: A Blueprint for Revitalizing the Manufacturer-Supplier Partnership* (New York: AMACOM, 1989). Reproduced with permission.

3. Project priorities, based on ROI, savings, urgency, ease of solution, or permanence of benefits.
4. Steering committees to guide projects and diagnostic teams to tackle projects.
5. Diagnosis: from symptom, to cause, to solution.
6. Breakthrough in cultural resistance to change: identifying cultural patterns threatened and extending ownership to members of the culture in planning and executing the change.
7. Breakthrough in results: reduced inspection and reduced costs of quality.

Cycle Time

Cycle time measures the time span between identification of a need (for a purchased material/service) and receipt of the full value of that material or service. This measure requires the supply manager to identify all the steps between need identification and receipt of the final value, including designing, ordering, testing, specifying, bidding, scheduling, actual use of the material/service, the flow of information, measurement/feedback time, and, finally, payment to the supplier. Cycle time steps are identified by use of a value chain map. The cycle time measure is key to focusing on improving your ability to transfer new features and benefits from the supplier into your work system to create value for your customer. Hence, less time is better. This is the simple essence of time-based competition: The fastest will win.

Not only is cycle time an important measure in lessening development time for new products and services, it is equally important as a strategic competitive factor in the manufacturing or delivery cycle for both new and existing products. Time required is an indicator of process complexity, so if a concentrated effort is made to reduce cycle time, the process must be simplified, reducing resources and costs at the same time. It has also been shown that these simpler processes are less error-prone, thus improving quality as well.

The information needed in cycle time measure is a time accounting of all the steps in the cycle, including total time for each work step plus the waiting time between steps. The measure is used to evaluate material/service stream effectiveness before and after each iteration of reengineering or redesign. The continual improvement process and the measure of cycle time will always reduce this cycle time.

"Should Cost" Analysis

"Should Cost" analysis measures periodic changes in the marketplace technology and their impact on the fundamental material or service cost structure. It is the inductive look at how outside factors, changes in the economy, labor rates, technology, and information are helping suppliers alter their costs. The figure arrived at in "should cost" analysis becomes the "ideal cost target" for the cash cost.

Price analysis and cost analysis have been part of the procurement literature for some time. Many should-cost analysis texts are available. A particularly good analysis, from Burt and Pinkerton's *Strategic Proactive Procurement*, is shown in Figure 9-2.

Cash cost and "should cost" are the measures that allow the supply manager to optimize acquisition costs by revealing the ideal cost target. Of course, they require conducting periodic analysis—they can't be tracked daily or monthly—but there is no other way to collect an understanding of the ideal cost as a target for improvement.

(text continues on page 193)

Figure 9-2. Special secondary source techniques for estimating cost components.

Assuming the supplier will not reveal the cost component breakdowns and if the buyer has little or no internal cost accounting help or cost element knowledge, secondary sources can help the buyer derive the individual cost components of a proposed price and do it with an adequate degree of accuracy. Annual reports, 10K SEC Supplements, the *Annual U.S. Industrial Outlook,* Dun & Bradstreet reports, and other studies such as *Dun's Financial Record™,* the *Prentice-Hall Annual Almanac of Business and Financial Ratios,* Robert Morris Associates annual statements studies in Philadelphia, Moody's Industrials, Standard & Poor Data, Value Line, and the *U.S. Census of Manufacturers,* plus numerous other U.S. documents and documents from the Bureau of Labor Statistics contain cost-revealing data. There are a variety of databases such as Dialog in Palo Alto, California; CompuServe in Columbus, Ohio; Nexis (in most libraries); Dow Jones Quick Search; in addition to database directories such as Database Directory and DataBasics.[1]

One such derivative method is the one originated by Newman and Scodro.[2] If the analyst knows the supplier's product Standard Industrial Classification Code (SIC), which is listed in Dun & Bradstreet reports, the 1982 U.S. SIC Directory, all U.S. Census reports, and most industrial directories, he or she can work "backward" as per the following illustration:

Price per unit: $20.00 (from supplier's proposal-quote)
Material to labor ratio: 5 to 1 (from the *U.S. Census of Manufacturers*)
Cost of goods sold (COGS): 76% of sales (from the annual report or *Dun's Financial Record*)
SC&A Expenses: 15% of sales (from the annual report or Dun's credit report)
Net income: 9% of sales (from the annual report or Dun's credit report)
Material to sales ratio: 35% of sales (from the *U.S. Census of Manufacturers*)

By converting, we derive the following:

Material costs	=	35% of $20	=	$7.00
Direct labor is 100/5	=	20% of $7	=	1.40
Overhead (76% – 35% – 7%)	=	34% of $20	=	6.80
SG&A	=	15% of $20	=	3.00
Net Income	=	9% of $20	=	1.80
		TOTAL PRICE		$20.00

Using these figures and other sources such as those already cited plus the buyer's estimates, we can determine which cost elements are out of line when compared to industry benchmarks as well as the total price.

Another such derivative method that produces a "should cost" price or cost model is a type of benchmark method proposed by Burt, Norquist, and Anklesaria.[3] We will use an example of a material intensive electronic component:

Price per unit, $20.00
From the supplier's proposal-quote

Material cost based on 30% of price or sales	=	$6.00	From the U.S. Census or Annual Survey of Manufacturers
Direct labor based on a material to labor ratio of 11.31 to 1 or 100/11.31 = 8.8% x $6.00	=	.53	From the U.S. Census or Annual Survey of Manufacturers
Factory overhead at 175% of direct labor	=	.93	
Total Factory Cost	=	$7.46	
SG&A at 31.8% of factory cost	=	$2.37	From the Annual Statement Studies, Robert Morris Associates
Total Cost	=	9.83	
Profit is $20.00 – 9.83	=	$10.17	

(continues)

Figure 9-2. *(continued)*

Note that the profit of $10.17 is 103% of total cost v. the normal industry profit rate of 25% (from the annual statement studies). These statement studies indicate that a normal profit should be $2.46 for an expected price per unit of $12.29 (total cost: $9.83 plus profit of 2.46 = $12.29). We now have an excellent agenda item for the negotiation meeting as the profit is way too high unless we have asked for some very special requirement involving very high risk for the supplier. In addition, because we estimated material cost at 30% of the quoted price of $20.00 with this abnormal profit component, the realistic price could be in the $9.00 range as we would now start the process with a much lower price than $20.00.

Presenting our estimate to the supplier team will usually provoke a detailed counter-response and at the least, will stimulate a vigorous debate and possible concession unless the component is unique and in very high demand with unusual terms and conditions. In any event, "should cost" models provide the incentive and documentation to explore cost component breakdowns. One other caution: Price is just one part of total cost, which means pure price quotes are actually inadequate indicators of total costs, or total cost of ownership (TCO).

"Should cost" and other derivative type models also identify the key cost drivers and reveal what cost elements are out of line with industry benchmarks. Is it labor, material, overhead, or profit? This analysis also begs the question of "are our specifications too high or is the supplier capability too low?" Do not pay for unnecessary requirements or for services not used or needed. If the supplier is charging high engineering overhead for a part the buyer designed, this cost component should be reduced or eliminated.

Finally, will cost analysis always reduce costs to a reasonable level? "No" is the answer as we always face the supply-demand issue. For example, in the late fall of 1994, several major aluminum producers obtained price increases of approximately 50 percent from large can manufacturers.[4] This price increase resulted from high demand and short supply for can sheet and uniform price increases by all major can sheet suppliers. The price increase was led by Alcoa, which announced that all can customers would have to pay the London Metal Exchange price for aluminum ingot. While such a "peg" could also lower the price in the future, the only actions the can producers have available is to pay the higher price or substitute another material.

Notes

1. See Richard G. Newman, *Supplier Price Analysis: A Guide for Purchasing, Accounting, and Financial Analysts* (Westport, Conn.: Quorum Books, a division of Greenwood Press, 1992), pp. 51–73. Reprinted with permission of Greenwood Publishing Group, Inc., Westport, Conn. Copyright © 1992.
2. Richard G. Newman and J. Scodro, "Price Analysis for Negotiation," *Journal of Purchasing and Materials Management* (Spring 1988), pp. 8–15.
3. David N. Burt, Warren E. Norquist, and Jimmy Anklesaria, *Zero Based Pricing™: Achieving World Class Competitiveness Through Reduced All-in-Costs* (Chicago, Ill.: Probus, 1990), pp. 143–173.
4. Norton Erle, "Aluminum Makers Pushing Through Price Increases to Can Manufacturers," *The Wall Street Journal* (November 18, 1994), p. A2.

From: David N. Burt and Richard L. Pinkerton, *A Purchasing Manager's Guide to Strategic Proactive Procurement* (New York: AMACOM, 1996). Reprinted with permission.

The four definitive measures of material/service stream effectiveness are shown in Figure 9-3. They are the measures necessary for every supply stream. The information to be tracked, of course, is specific to each material or service stream. Each supply manager or supply team must decide which information is to be tracked to create these measures. These measures should be reviewed at least quarterly.

Figure 9-3. Key measures of material/service stream effectiveness.

Cash Costs Total Cost Cycle Time Should Cost	>	Material/Service Stream Measures of Effectiveness

Supply Management Process Effectiveness

Separate from the issue of the effectiveness of the material or service supply-stream strategy is the issue of whether or not all the people using this material or service are employing this supply-stream strategy to change. The supply management core processes are designed to *create and implement* strategies. Ultimately, all the continual improvements, the innovation, even the savings in cash costs or employee time can be realized only if purchasing behavior and usage behavior are changed. These changes occur only if the implementation step in these core processes is effective, and usage behavior is actually changed.

Therefore, the second critical measure must deal with the implementation and effectiveness of the supply management process itself. Are people doing the right thing? Is it coming together? Are the results those expected?

Specifically, two performance measures are required:

1. Have the supply-stream strategy and the supply management process delivered the specified supply-stream requirements?
2. What percentage of total purchases and total usage are implementing the new supply strategy with preferred suppliers?

In great part, these measures indicate internal user satisfaction. In this case, however, you are not surveying for *internal customer "happiness"* with procurement personnel, just some general notion of overall satisfaction. Rather, you want to know:

1. Did we deliver the identified requirements?

2. How many users are implementing the preferred strategy?

Table 9-2 shows the information you need to track to determine these measures.

Table 9-2. Supply management process effectiveness.

Specific Performance Measure	Information for Tracking
1. Satisfaction of requirements	— On-time/complete delivery/quality acceptance, etc. — Product/service performance vis-à-vis specifications Price deviations Quantity deviations
2. Percentage of total purchases consolidated with preferred suppliers	— Purchase analysis per supply stream

To determine whether or not you are meeting specified requirements, tracking information must be directly associated with specific requirements, as shown in Table 9-2. At minimum, you want to ensure that materials and services were received, as planned. Optimally, you want evaluation levels for satisfaction of requirements and expected benefits. These measures include:

- On-time/complete delivery statistics
- Product/service performance per specifications
- Benefits delivered as expected
- Pricing and quantity that meet specified orders

Overall Process Effectiveness

Overall process effectiveness is a measure of being able to implement material/service strategies. Simply put, Have you been able to convince internal users to switch suppliers and product/service usage patterns? The measures of this behavior are the percentage of total purchases made with the preferred suppliers and the percentage of usage patterns conforming with the specified strategy. Obviously, if the "subscription rate" is low, a new implementation plan is required. If it is high, the users become a fertile community for learning and introducing ideas for improvement.

Overall Competitive Effectiveness

Because the entire purpose of the supply management process is to create competitive advantage from dollars spent on purchased materials and services, the final test is simply: Have we in fact achieved competitive advantage, and how do we measure this by material stream? You do this by comparing yourself with your competitors in four key areas:

1. Purchase prices for comparable materials and services
2. Purchase practices
3. Supply management practices
4. Key suppliers

Benchmarking is the key to this comparison. This is such an important tool, so critical to your success, that we need to take a minute here to develop this a little further.

Entire texts, available at your library or bookstore, have been published on this topic, so we won't develop an academic treatise on the subject here, but it is important to highlight a few areas for clarification.

Many use the terms *benchmarking* and *best practices* synonymously. They aren't synonyms. Benchmarking is systematic and ongoing. It generally refers to assessing your organization's needs for improvement by telephoning or visiting businesses within your own industry or even in other industries (often greater expertise is found *outside* your industry in similar functional processes) that you believe to be "best in class" in given work processes or in supporting customers or products.

It does not refer to "what" but to "how" a specific supply-stream process compares to a "best in class" process.

Best practices is actually a part of benchmarking. It is the way leading business operations implement work processes well. Sharing best practices is not benchmarking—only the sharing of good ideas. Trolling for best practices may prove beneficial but without the complete understanding of the work process and clearly identified process boundaries, it is incomplete and marginally beneficial.

Benchmarking is conducted through the following sources:

- Government and commercial literature
- Industry associations/industry experts
- Suppliers
- Best-in-class companies
- Consultants/custom research firms

A search of government and commercial literature will help you to get background material and understand the leading-edge technology and practices as well as vital industry statistics and industry leaders. Specific examples of useful publications include the following:

- Annual reports with key financial data
- U.S. Department of Commerce *Census of Manufacturers,* which contains statistics on manufacturing overheads
- U.S. Department of Commerce *Annual Survey of Manufacturers,* containing ratios of material to labor for manufactured products
- *Purchasing Magazine,* which publishes quarterly commodity transaction prices

Industry associations and experts can provide general literature to allow you to understand key material or service trends. Industry associations can also refer you to industry leaders, suppliers, and experts.

Suppliers can give you a good idea of which of their customers are leading-edge companies. **Ask your best suppliers who their best customers are and then visit them.** Suppliers can often describe opportunities you may wish to pursue. Find out about the supplier's industry technology. How is it applied and used? How is it best consumed? How is it administered? How is it measured?

Leading-edge companies in almost all industry segments usually have high stock price multiples and generate a fair amount of industry acclaim. Trace their overall process fundamentals. Find out what drives their strategy. Identify specific practices and processes to benchmark. Invite top operating management to speak, or interview them if possible.

Custom research firms and consultants provide benchmarking information for a fee. This can run $25,000 to $75,000, depending on complexity, so it should probably be reserved for key materials and services and done at regular, but infrequent, intervals. Omnibus market segment studies (e.g., on flexible packaging, copper cable) are also available. Your supply management leaders can commission or otherwise avail themselves of market research data, specifically, market segment behaviors or specific supplier practices. Tailored market studies for smaller commodity or market segments are available and affordable. Organizations devoted specifically to the purchasing function, such as the Center for Advanced Purchasing Studies and the National Association of Purchasing Management, can provide cost benchmarks and leading-edge-practice philosophies.

Kaiser Associates is a well-known research organization that specializes in developing competitive intelligence. The company serves Fortune 500 clients by providing strategic and financial summaries of key competitors (or key suppliers) along with an analysis of the implications for the client's business strategy. It also provides specific purchase cost benchmarks for materials and services. Many corporations subscribe to this type of ongoing competitive benchmarking for purchases, including major corporations in consumer products, telecommunications, and, especially, general manufacturing.

The purpose of this benchmarking is to close the gap between your company and your best competition by constructing a "could be" model detailing the following:

- Shortest material flow
- Best practices/best technology, including best purchasing and supply management practices
- Most competitiveness
- Best administration and measurement
- "Should cost," including purchase price for comparable materials and services
- Best suppliers

Benchmarking can provide a clear sense of how your processes and skills rate compared to those of your best competitors.

The Measurement Process

You should periodically take time to measure your supply management strategies to gather information that will help the supply manager adjust the implementation plan for the overall supply management process. This adjustment may take several forms:

- Altering the strategy
- Reallocating resources
- Removing barriers
- Introducing new capabilities

The prime value of the measurement process derives from the opportunity to review progress and share learning among those individuals responsible for implementing the strategy: supply managers and team participants, supplier personnel, and operating or business personnel who are the actual users of the purchased materials and services. Table 9-3 shows the information that you need to collect and the management activities required for the measurement process and their frequency as well as who should be responsible for those tasks.

Since many of the measurements you establish will be new, be prepared for resistance. "Measurement blockers" are dealt with effectively in the March 1996 American Management Association's *Management Review.* John H. Lingle and William A. Schiemann suggest that fuzzy ob-

Table 9-3. Management activities and supporting information for the measurement process.

Responsible Party	Monthly	Quarterly	Annually
Supply Stream Manager	■ Invoice pricing ■ Inventory levels ■ Process compliance ■ Usage statistics ■ Benchmarking	■ Recap price, process, and usage performance ■ Review of changes to process or usage practices	■ Recap progress vis-à-vis continual improvement plan ■ Review changes in total cost of ownership analysis ■ Develop next annual improvement plan
Supply Team Members	■ Track progress of process changes ■ Measure usage effectiveness ■ Measure purchase exceptions to preferred supplier	■ Recap process changes ■ Review usage improvements ■ Review process improvements	■ Recap suppliers' resource effectiveness ■ Review inputs to total cost model ■ Determine inputs to next annual plan

(continues)

Table 9-3. (*continued*)

Procurement Head	■ Review recap of progress and process change by supply stream ■ Recognize outstanding performance	■ Review progress of annual plans ■ Review next annual plan ■ Recognize performance of supply teams and suppliers
Supplier Personnel	■ Implement process changes in flow or transactions ■ Implement usage practices ■ Measure improvements	■ Track progress vis-à-vis project plan for all changes ■ Review usage measures versus best industry benchmarks	■ Recap annual performance ■ Develop opportunities for improvement ■ Review resourse support for next year

The measurement process is essential to material and service stream learning, and should be incorporated into each stream's implementation plan.

jectives, unjustified trust in informal feedback systems, entrenched measurement systems, and the activity trap are all blockers.

Make sure the objectives of supply management are clear. If users, internal or external, are vague about these expectations, make sure they define goals and objectives. Ask how the results can be measured for all supply streams.

Also look at entrenched measures that may simply no longer be relevant. Don't fall into the trap of measuring activity—the number of purchase orders placed, the number of events, and so on. These types of measures are irrelevant to understanding actual usage effectiveness and overall competitive effectiveness.

Currently, organizations do not have formal mechanisms for sharing measurement information. At best, the procurement buyer may share some anecdotal feedback with the supplier, usually after a problem has occurred.

Table 9-3 provides the role definition for participants in the supply management process showing the specific tasks and information required to make the process effective.

The measurement process should be used as a thoughtful, periodic review of progress toward your goals and as a forum to discuss necessary change. (This process should never be confused with—or be regarded as a substitute for—information tracking or an on-line data retrieval process.) There is no substitute for management involvement for successfully implementing supply management. The benefits of the measurement process are the management focus, information sharing, and learning and adjusting action accordingly.

Implementation Guide

This one will be easy. This chapter provides the specific information and activities required to measure supply management effectiveness. Are these measurements in place? Do your people seem to understand the purpose of a supply management strategy, and do they see the connection to these measurements?

Remember:

1. How effective is the individual supply-stream strategy in maximizing value for your dollars spent? Do you believe the strategy is contributing directly to your cost control? Are you getting real interchange with your new, focused supply base? Is that interchange leading to new technology faster than previously experienced? Are your suppliers creative people contributing to your *mutual* success? Are you using the right technology (products, services, capabilities)? Are you using it in the right way?

Key Measures of Supply Management Effectiveness and Tracking Information

- Acquisition costs
- Total cost of ownership
- Cycle time
- "Should cost"
- Invoiced pricing and inventories
- Usage measures and supporting costs
- Total elapsed time
- Periodic analysis

2. How effective is the supply management process in implementing that strategy? Is everyone in your business

using the strategy? Who isn't? Why? Are most of the dollars covered? Are the critical products included?

3. How effective is the supply-stream strategy compared to your competitors' strategy for the same material or service? Do you think that you are getting products to market faster than your competition? Do you believe that your products and services are enjoying greater customer acceptance than your competitors'—from surveys, public data, benchmarking?

Do your supply managers have the skills and determination to carry out their role? Do you—and they—understand what they are accountable for? Are they willing to do the telephone and face-to-face interviewing? Are they giving you the necessary technical documentation? Can they do the cost analysis work? This is an ongoing process—are your supply managers identifying ongoing updates?

In the final analysis, you should be able to benchmark your material stream costs, your usage practices, and your material and service cycle times for your critical or high-cost supply streams relative to your competitors'. If your individual supply-stream strategies do not produce better results than those of your strongest competitors, you have little chance of competitive advantage for your *overall* products or services.

Whatever you do, capture the measured value. Change the business model to capitalize on it!

- If large savings, either direct or indirect, are realized, reduce the corresponding operating budgets. Don't let these savings be absorbed by an internal department.

- If supplier cycle time is reduced, apply it to the marketing plan. Don't let time slip to a downstream internal function.
- When these kinds of benefits occur, market them to Wall Street as a fundamental change to realize competitive advantage being developed.

CHAPTER 10

Secrets to Success

Implementing the widespread use of a major new business process can be viewed as either profoundly simple or so ominously complex that it succumbs to the weight of all its objections. Our experience has taught us that strong leadership can provide the focus necessary to "Keep It Simple." At the end of the day, a new process is composed of some standard concepts and skills that are broadly applied to achieve the objectives of the process. Garnering acceptance of the pertinent concepts and compliance in consistently applying these concepts is the complex part of the supply management implementation journey. When these concepts are routinely applied, however, they produce consistent, reproducible results.

The "complex" part of the trip: the changing of human opinion and behavior.

Coming from the brute-force era of mandated policies and programs, we personally have learned to adjust quickly to these leadership signals even if silently questioning purpose and outcomes. The same forces that gave rise to the power of individuals and teams (see Chapter 2) also opened the door to permissive cultures and work environments. This rather massive shift in attitude challenges the discipline of old hierarchical leadership styles, with

207

employees almost demanding your proof of purpose before they will agree to comply. It's easy for leaders to say "If they don't like it here, they can leave," but, practically speaking, that's just plain ridiculous.

Thus, the perilous part of this journey demands proof and demonstration of the seriousness of your intent. Said another way, it's time to let your actions speak louder than your words. We believe these actions are your secrets to success and will reverberate throughout your organization.

These actions require you to demonstrate your purpose in four ways:

1. Communicate the "mental shifts" in what is valued.
2. Recognize individual and team models of success.
3. Share learning with other organizations.
4. Provide ongoing formal communication to internal and external stakeholders.

Communicating the Key "Mental Shifts"

Let's face it, the supply management concepts are based on a new set of rules. Under these new rules, thinking and behavior will shift in many ways:

- Procurement personnel shift from the role of narrowly focused buyer to that of multidimensional supply leader.
- Buyers become internal product managers, and the focus of work shifts from performing routine tasks to creating long-term value.
- Functional leaders shift from a manager/supervisor role to that of coach, providing focus on the path forward.

- Executive managers shift from the role of book-keeper/scorekeeper to that of leader, with emphasis on creating an environment of motivation and learning.
- The work environment evolves from one that is procedurally bound and tightly controlled to one that is empowering, open, and focused on managing processes.
- Processes shift from discrete functions to integrated, cross-functional, cross-business interactions.
- Systems shift from standardized transaction-processing mechanisms to customized vehicles for meeting end customers' needs.
- Structure shifts from hierarchical organizational layers to horizontal networks and teams that span business units and functions.

Underneath all these mental and behavioral shifts is a fundamental change in beliefs and values: new beliefs in maximizing "functional" productivity, not protecting turf; new beliefs about the goal of competitive advantage, the role of total cost, and the need for continual improvement. These beliefs culminate in a significant tangible new metric, which will forever change your supply side annual planning: the recognition that these practices create negative inflation.

We can remember working with a group of supply teams, who consistently demonstrated a range of supply-stream benefits during a two-year period—including hard-cash savings in price, inventory elimination, and so on. Yet, at the beginning of this organization's next budget cycle, these supply leaders were customarily polled for price projections on their supply-stream areas in the upcoming business planning year. Automatically, they all submitted budgets reflecting a 3 to 5 percent increase in the new year.

In fact, rarely should prices rise, unless some fundamental economic or market shift is the cause. The very nature of the continual improvement work is armed to reduce total cost.

Simply, the ultimate financial shifts require new goals of *negative inflation* and *zero supply inventories.*

These shifts in thinking and behavior can be traced to five "new values" that are the underpinnings of the supply management system:

1. *Achieving optimum total cost of ownership will maximize the value of a supply stream.* Although you don't want to focus exclusively on the acquisition cost, it *is* important. Competitively advantaged suppliers will reward you for your consolidated purchases with acquisition cost benefits as well as with help in optimizing TCO. Simply put, you're after it all—low acquisition cost and lowest total cost. Only the "best suppliers" can help you attain these goals.

2. *Benchmarking "best practices" is the fuel of continual improvement.* Ongoing benchmarking of best supply-stream practices creates new ideas and opportunities for continual improvement. Moreover, it provides a necessary link to the ever changing marketplace as a source of opportunities for improvement and innovation. Without these links, supply practices would become stagnant within two years. Therefore, benchmarking the practices of other organizations becomes a way of life for the supply team and a valuable work input. These tasks require time and budget support or they will be squeezed out of the supply team's work. This marketplace link is the cornerstone of cost improvement work.

3. *Learning has value.* Ongoing optimization processes foster continual change. With change come success and failure. Generally, we learn from our failures, not our successes, yet the cultural norm is to reward only success. The supply teams must have the permission to try new solutions *and* fail. The majority of unsuccessful changes we see implemented cause only minor delays or disruptions when they fail. Certainly nothing that can't be repaired or regained. The idea is to learn from failure, not punish people for trying new ideas for improvement. The messages to support this learning philosophy must be demonstrative; otherwise, the "cover our always perfect aspect" will remain the company norm.

4. *Performance measurement requires hard metrics.* Supply management concepts are analytical tools to help supply leaders craft strategies for improvement. These strategies are based on developing hard metrics of effectiveness. These include all dimensions of total cost, usage, time, process effectiveness, and on. Measurement takes time and effort on the part of the supply team. Baldrige Award winners consistently implore customers to evaluate performance in tangible terms. This feedback is vital to their improvement. No matter how elegant or flashy the strategy or how large the promise of benefit, the truth is in "what happened." The key information required to measure supply-stream effectiveness, supply management process effectiveness, and overall competitive effectiveness is covered in Chapter 9. If you consistently require the same hard metrics to describe a supply stream's effectiveness, then measuring as an activity will become integrated into the fabric of supply team work.

5. *Time.* Simply, how long did it take you? How long until you'll see improvements? Who has the best time?

What time does your customer need? Your support of this new value moves an organization from a planning style to an implementation focus. A "Just do it!" organization values time and learning as the mainstay of their work. These signals of new value must come from you.

Recognizing Models of Results

The easiest way to effect a desired shift in what is valued is to establish new role models. When you formally hold up a new role model, it forces observers to check what signals you are sending.

Recognizing new role models can take a number of forms, including acknowledging who did what and how they did it. While it is important to recognize which individuals and teams made what specific achievements, it is equally critical to recognize *how* they did so. The "how" is the learning model for your organization, representing the assimilation of the concepts that you've been trying to establish. It provides the opportunity to define the "intangible" values while pointing to the hard achievements. For example, recognizing a supply team for a significant change in acquisition cost and subsequent usage reductions clearly reports hard results, particularly if you can point to definitive numbers (e.g., 18 percent cost saving and 5 percent usage reduction).

But going on to describe how they worked—"They completely discarded the past, were willing to rethink the entire supplier base, sought out leading-edge usage practices, and put it all together in one grand plan. Moreover, they actually made it happen. These are all the intangibles. They involved the right people, they took no prisoners, and now we'll all benefit"—you share learning about how they worked and why it has value.

From this formal recognition of role models, listeners will take away a multitude of messages, not the least of which is that you value initiative, speed, creativity, boldness, careful involvement of the right people, and sheer determination. We believe it is a lot more meaningful to talk about these intangible values with real examples than to simply recite a list of such desired characteristics, which can be perceived as a wish for the unrealistic. People will do heroic things if given the motivation, the skills, and the permission. Role model recognition is an efficient way to spread the word while at the same time formally acknowledging results. Those who have actually delivered hard results will strive for new standards of excellence and begin to provide informal leadership for others in the organization. In effect, recognizing role models is like tossing a pebble into a still pond. It sends out a series of concentric rings, each touching another.

Two types of work achievement merit recognition:

1. *Creation of new supply-stream models.* New supply-stream models are key to providing the learning needed by the supply management organization. These models may involve different market leverage approaches, new usage practices, dramatic streamlining of material flows, or creating accelerated time cycles for improvements. Recognition of these models provides the opportunity to showcase the individuals involved and share the results of their actual problem solving and creativity.

2. *Successful implementation of supply-stream models.* Successful implementation models are equally important because they reinforce the point that implementation is the critical step in achieving the end result. Strategies are great

but must be translated into action quickly. Implementing change is not an easy task. Those individuals who overcome the dragon of inertia and lead others to new, better methods of use are leaders in their own right. Your recognition reinforces the value, Change is good.

Recognizing positive accomplishments should include spotlighting barriers that the supply team overcame. These barriers need not have personal names but rather may be descriptions of the types of organizational resistance encountered. These include all forms of protectionism that impede progress and collaboration, as well as the disease of risk aversion, which permeates organizational cultures and delays change indefinitely.

Supply management teams will thrive in an atmosphere that recognizes implementation determination even after an occasional failure or setback. It is far better to have pressed the envelope and lost the case for a new supply model than to be so risk averse as not to try.

Recognition is almost as important as rewards, but obviously if you can do both you can multiply the impact. In one consultation, we scheduled quarterly sessions to review progress and achievements. We selected role models of learning and implementation from this review and formally recognized the results in an open forum of the supply management organization. The teams or individuals were asked to share their learning on videotapes, which were circulated to all locations.

In addition to this recognition, they received $1,000–$2,000 bonus achievement awards for their performance. This program set the stage for management expectations and values and delivered tangible proof of achievement being rewarded with both recognition and dollars. This effort was one of our most significant motivators of group performance.

Share Learning

"By the time the outside world begins recognizing your successes, you know you really have something." Or so the adage reads. But for supply management, outside recognition is key to attracting best suppliers and experts to work with your organization. Rather than wait for news of your successes to reach the outside world, why not take your learning platform to your supply base and network of experts? By sharing your models of success with the supply community, you set the same expectations for performance as you do with your supply management organization. This becomes your opportunity to share your achievements and expectations to become a "best customer" dealing with best suppliers, within the context of a "learning agenda," which precludes being accused of bragging or manipulating. In effect, you are creating a learning forum that encourages suppliers to offer other practices or strategies that your organization may have missed. Moreover, it reinforces your desire for proactive supply management proposals from suppliers.

There are at least three ways we know to create this learning forum:

1. Annual supplier meetings
2. Supplier roundtables
3. Supplier workshops

Annual Supplier Meetings

Many companies have annual supplier meetings, such as golf outings or more formal affairs to provide a forum for new direction and corporate communication. We recommend using the annual supplier meeting as a teaching and learning platform and as an opportunity to distinguish your organization as a supply management leader. This type of meeting begins with a review of your organization's supply management performance, learning, and future goals. The centerpiece of the meeting, however, is real learning about key supply strategies that support your business.

We once conducted this type of meeting for a large paper products manufacturer. The three supply-stream strategies we singled out for presentation all involved eliminating time-consuming, non-value-adding work tasks that absorbed a huge amount of employee time. These major supply-stream areas included maintenance, repair and operating supplies, general and administration supplies and services, and the procurement and payments processes. The suppliers were presented actual case studies of learning, including the before-and-after supply strategy approaches. We highlighted the benefits realized, especially the time and dollars saved. The suppliers were left with a template of these same strategies to assess how they might help them to redesign their purchase streams. One hundred fifty of the 175 suppliers invited to this meeting sent follow-up letters requesting information for their supply management organizations.

Some companies use supplier meetings to bring in experts in leading-edge topics.

Annual supplier meetings require extensive planning and some expense. They create a highly visible platform for leadership messages, however. You are after all addressing the leaders of leading businesses in this hemisphere. Such visibility is critical in shaping external perceptions about your organization and your leadership ability.

Supplier Roundtables

Supplier roundtables are a more informal way to accomplish shared learning. The roundtable provides the opportunity to invite seven to ten supplier representatives, preferably the chief executive or chief operating officers or other relevant corporate officers for marketing, research, or supply management. The roundtable discussion parallels the annual supplier meeting agenda, beginning with your review of your organization's progress and goals along with a description of key strategy shifts and major kernels of learning. You lead subsequent discussion by polling practices of the supplier organizations in improving cycle time to market or new innovation techniques. These topics provide the opportunity for a collaborative discussion without forcing participants into a "show and tell" performance.

The main benefits of these forums derive more from the direction that participants will pass on to the supplier organization after the roundtable, again reinforcing the need for proactive supply-stream management proposals. The supplier roundtable can work at several levels within your organization, including executive roundtables, technical roundtables, supply management roundtables, all with a shared learning agenda. This mechanism is informal and flexible and can be tailored to meet the style of the business leader host. Finally, it builds a base of trust and respect, which is fundamental to a successful supplier relationship.

Supplier Workshops

Supplier workshops are aimed at creating opportunities for supply-stream innovation that will benefit all participants.

This forum is composed of supplier participants who provide materials and services that are critical to the products your organization brings to the marketplace. For example, a leader of a consumer products business might invite a chemical producer, packaging manufacturer, process equipment provider, information systems expert, and product designer to meet and share best industry practices for a given product type. The discussion format centers on what magnitude of change in process is necessary to provide a goal of, say, five times the functional benefit for one-half the current cost.

Such a provocative question signals a search for real departures in approach and opens the door for a new type of collaboration. The workshop brainstorming can be used to generate more focused follow-up sessions if real interest in new approaches develops. This concept is one of the many fast-innovation prototyping methods being used to shorten the sequential planning cycle that leads to product development.

The discussion and brainstorming methods and techniques are all pretty standard. They need the right combination of participants along with your leadership to focus the discussion on innovation in order to create new opportunities. Like the roundtables, these supplier workshops can be created to include various functional competencies and different levels of expertise. Following are typical workshop participants:

Hosting Business Organization	*Supplier Participants*	*Outside Experts*
Business heads	Business heads	Systems experts
Business leaders	Marketing leaders	Product designers
Marketing leaders	R&D leaders	

Product development leaders	Manufacturing leaders	Process technology experts
Manufacturing leaders		
R&D leaders		
Supply management leaders		

These workshop sessions can draw upon the continual innovation process and concepts to provide the structure necessary to guide and organize discussion and work sessions. In this way, you can look to your supply leaders to organize and facilitate the sessions and summarize the results and next steps. The business leaders who learn to use these collaborative forums for creating new opportunity will unlock a new wave of competitive advantage in which all participants can share the gains.

Formal Communication Plans

We've talked throughout the book about the role of communication and leadership in successfully implementing the supply management process. Simply put, regular communication is the vital language of leadership. From our experience, you simply cannot overcommunicate. Furthermore, your plans for communication should embrace all audiences of people who will be affected by the supply management change or its benefits, including those stakeholders external to your business.

The purpose of a formal communication plan is to market the benefits and features of the new supply management process in order to create understanding, en-lightenment, and proactive participation in the process.

NYNEX Telecommunications (now Bell Atlantic) has led a highly successful revamping of its supplier base and procurement processes with the skillful use of aggressive communication. The supply management leader created a high-level team within the organization to not only create a strategy for NYNEX but also package and merchandise the message to all NYNEX employees far and wide. The net result was a massive shift in behavior resulting in fewer suppliers, dollar savings, new work practices, and a new positioning for future continual improvement work.

You too will want to develop a communication plan, remarkably similar in purpose to your advertising plans for the products and services your business markets. Specifically, this communication plan will target three objectives:

1. Build broad awareness and understanding of the supply management process and its key benefits.
2. Implement the new processes.
3. Engage relevant participants in leadership by specific supply-stream management.

The communication plan should be developed to span a twelve-month period coincidental with your planning cycle and your supply management goals. During this period every audience should receive multiple messages in varied formats in order to develop a familiarity and understanding about the new way to procure materials and services.

These target audiences span all your business constituents, including:

Internal	External
■ Procurement	■ Suppliers (key executives)
■ Customer operating units	■ Suppliers' functional resources
■ Shared resource groups	■ Suppliers' employees
■ Executive leaders	■ Industry associations
■ Specific pilot teams (as they form)	■ Shareholders
■ Key functional audiences (who will participate regularly, e.g., accounts payable, maintenance)	
■ All other employees, at all locations	

A separate data file of names and addresses should be created to provide easy delivery of communication plan messages. The plan itself consists of creating a specific message for each audience, highlighting relevant benefits and features. So while certain brochures or flyers may be created for all audiences, these can be customized by target audience with personalized cover notes.

The communication plan content should deliver three campaign messages during a twelve- to eighteen-month period. Such messages might include the following:

Introduction to Supply Management	How to Use the New Process and Participant's Role	Specific Supply-Stream Strategies and Benefits
■ Explanation of the difference between supply management and procurement	■ Restatement of purpose and benefits	■ Introducing major new supply-stream features and benefits

- What it is and how it works
- Key benefits for
    Your organization
    Individual employees
    Business leaders
    Shared-resource groups
- What will happen next
- Benefits of supplier consolidation

- How to access the supply process to secure purchased materials
- How to participate in key supply streams
- New skills required
- Specific new procedures and work flow changes

- Descriptions of supply-stream models and success stories, with tangible results
- Interviews with employees and process participants

Each audience should receive customized communications in various formats dealing with these key messages. Possible formats for these messages include the following:

- Personal memo/mailings
- E-mail
- Voice mail
- Face-to-face presentations
- Brochures
- Flyers/tent cards
- Videotapes
- Audiocassettes
- Closed-circuit TV
- Public relations

The communication master plan becomes a buildup of specific audience plans, which share some common messages and delivery vehicles.

An intensive communication plan is vital for this program's success. The communication plan, in conjunction with the capability-building plan (Chapter 8), becomes the primary strategy for creating and enabling change. Together they serve to inform the participants of supply management benefits, help them to apply concepts that generate tangible results, and encourage them to share learning, both successes and failures, so that they can make necessary changes.

Finally, successful implementation of a comprehensive communication plan guarantees success for your supply management process.

A final note about this secret to success is our belief in the value of consistency. We have seen countless corporate initiatives launched in our business careers. Most of these suffered a flash of early interest and a death of loving indifference. Those that survived and prospered benefited from constant leadership support, in words and deeds. The keys in this chapter are your tools to link your words and deeds as proof of your purpose and constancy.

IMPLEMENTATION GUIDE

Post the following keys to success in a place where you can review them regularly. Mark your calendar for specific activity dates (e.g., supplier meetings, workshops) and for times to review supply management progress in the areas indicated.

New Values in Thinking and Behavior

Optimum Total Cost of Ownership Will Maximize a
Supply-Stream Value
Best Practices "Fuel" Continuous Improvement
Learning Has Its Own Value
Measurement . . . Just the Facts
Time the New Dimension

Recognize Models of Learning and Results

Set Up Quarterly Reviews of Supply Management
Progress and Results
Identify, Recognize, and Reward Models of Achievement
in Two Areas:
Creation of New Supply-Stream Models
Successful Implementation of Supply-Stream Models

Provide for Broader Learning

Schedule the Following Mechanisms on Your Annual
Calendar:
Annual Supplier Meeting
Minimum of Four Supplier Roundtables
Two Supplier Workshops for Your Two Leading
Products/Services

Develop the Communication Plan

Identify Audiences, Internal and External

Engage Communications Resources to
Create Message Vehicles
(e.g., Flyers, Brochures)

Create Distribution/Mailing List

Build Specific Audience Plans

Engage Resources to Implement Plans

CHAPTER 11

Fast Forward

To master today's business challenges and opportunities, you need access to a wide array of special competencies to develop the quick solutions needed to remain competitive. Your supply management organization can provide this access. Supply teams have their fingers on the pulse of leading companies and their industries, understanding the impact of change on their capabilities and markets. These supply teams know the emerging products and services. They can establish the necessary links with market leaders to provide cost benefits, quality improvements, and competitive advantage that simply would not happen, relying solely on internal development paths and traditional relationships and structures. But your leadership is essential to make this happen. As Tom Peters said in *Pursuit of WOW* (1994), "People can smell emotional commitment from a mile away." Without this, you will fail.

We have described what it takes for the senior manager and supply leaders to be successful in this pursuit. We believe this opportunity becomes more and more vital as organizations continue to change size and shape. Limited organizational resources and skills will place an increasing demand on the marketplace to provide special competencies to fill these voids. The threat of increasing costs and the pressures of time will force businesses to reexamine these supply mechanisms and processes as they search for a new portal to marketplace solutions and new opportunities for competitive advantage.

The time is right, the path forward is clear, and the capabilities to begin already exist in your organization. So, have at it!

Suppose, for a moment, that you are the supply leader for your business.

It is two years from now, and you have successfully implemented a supply management process in your business. You are talking on the telephone with Dwight, your counterpart at another major corporation. He has called to inquire about your progress and success with suppliers.

> *Dwight:* But how did you do it? How did you get everyone to agree? How did you lead such a change in opinion and behavior in such a short time?
> *You:* It was easy. It took three standard processes, a little organization, and a few keys to success.
> *Dwight:* Oh, come on, you completely revamped the supply side of your business. Which consultants did you hire to implement your program?
> *You:* Why don't you visit with us for one day and see for yourself what is happening here? Only then will you believe what a little leadership and a lot of commitment can create.

You leave your office to meet new executives from one of your major suppliers. They too are interested in a broader view of how your supply management process works. They are anxious to watch your new business process in action. As you leave your office to greet your guests, you pass a conference room with new employees learning the fundamentals of total quality concepts. Two supply managers are leading the class, because quality issues have become a part of the new dialogue with suppliers and customers. You observe that the supply managers have become pretty good facilitators as a result of consistently working with cross-functional teams.

Approaching you in the hallway is Harry, a leader of one of the key business groups. Two years ago you would have walked across broken glass barefoot to avoid the encounter. Harry used to be a self-made expert who knew all the answers to his business unit's success, generally without the benefit of supporting facts. He was always lobbying for larger internal R&D because "you can't trust those suppliers" to come up with anything new. Life has changed for Harry over the last two years.

In discussing the development and launch of a new product line last week, you actually heard *him* say, "I didn't realize there were capabilities like that out there. At the rate that technology is moving, we can't possibly justify the investment to develop it when at least two of our best supply firms are already there. They have the technology. We can buy the capability for our products and actually take total cost out of the system." Two years ago, Harry couldn't spell "total cost."

Now he actually talks about total cost and can see the benefit of looking at all the costs in the system. He even followed up that conversation last week with a request to sit down and have a look at all the elements of his business that were consuming capital resources and human resources but were really not part of his business's core competencies.

"Hi, Harry."

"Hi. Looking forward to getting together Tuesday."

It never would have sounded like that in the old days.

Meanwhile, you are paged to take a call from the president's assistant, who is developing the agenda for the next strategic planning meeting in two weeks. You learn that the president has asked you to review the supply strategies for critical supply streams and the continual improvement plans with key suppliers. He has also asked that you review his planned remarks to a supplier consortium to ensure that he sends the right messages about continuing support to codevelopment and coengineering efforts for a new product line. The president's remarks include comments about the short development cycle that was possible during the last development project and preliminary indications that this can be improved even more with the current development effort.

The president's help has been significant, especially in the getting-started days of the supply management initiative. There were plenty of naysayers around, folks who were very comfortable with life as it was, and a fair number of outright saboteurs, the people who felt threatened by the idea of change. The president took the time to listen when you talked with him about the supply management opportunity. He asked for periodic updates as part of his regular staff meetings. He mentioned the effort in many of his quarterly video "chats" with associates.

When results began to be noticeable, he really became engaged. He quickly picked up on the potential for competitive advantage beyond simple cost control. He met with the senior management of your key supply companies and began to develop a high level of trust and collaboration. Between nine months and a year into implementing this process, he asked that supply management have a regular seat at the strategic planning reviews. That would have been unheard of in the old days. "Vendors" (lots of them) would have been involved well after the strategy had been determined, well after concepts had been developed, after specifications and schedules had been frozen. You're grateful those days are behind you and once again head for the lobby.

On the way, you also recall a recent meeting the president had with Wall Street analysts in which he credited supply management with the shorter time-to-market cycle and lower cost of operations. You unconsciously crack a smile.

You are meeting three key people from a company with which you are in the early stages of expanding a relationship. The company is a midsize conglomerate with some manufacturing and distribution divisions as well as a service division. The representatives were intrigued with the market analysis and selection process they participated in prior to being awarded a significant portion of your business. They want to learn more about implementing the supply management concepts within their business and with their suppliers. They indicated by phone when making this appointment that they pretty well understand these ideas for production materials and perhaps purchased goods generally, but are unclear how these concepts apply to indirect materials and services.

Their first questions were "How did you know where to start?" "How did you generate information on what was purchased and from which suppliers?" You begin a brief summary of the path traveled during the past two years (which bears a striking resemblance to chapters in this book). You highlight your supplier consolidation and procurement process reengineering work. But most of all you describe your organization as it works today:

- Flatter purchasing and supply management structures.
- A proliferation of cross-functional supply teams, dispersed throughout the organization.
- Linking supply chains from supplier's suppliers to the ultimate customer.
- Participation in key business and manufacturing processes.
- Ongoing capability building to hone a competitive competence in supply management.

You review characteristics and practices seen every day in the ongoing supply management work:

- A market/customer focus through ongoing analysis and benchmarking
- New methods and processes for supply-stream performance evaluation
- Total cost analysis in decision making
- Continual improvement plans for all supply-streams
- Reduction of transaction costs
- Ongoing focus on best practices for all supply stream usage
- Supplier alliance workshops aimed at improvement and innovation
- Emphasis on time-based strategies
- Strategic alignment with business and manufacturing plans

You conclude your remarks by highlighting specific opportunities for your visitors' service business. You emphasize that the opportunity is as great for service businesses as for manufacturers. The percentage reduction in acquisition cost for the goods and services needed to support a service enterprise may almost certainly be larger than comparable cost reductions in industrial businesses. Service enterprises have only recently begun to consolidate materials and services across the service enterprise. Their purchase has probably been relegated to the users of some of the services and support materials and with little strategic linking of key users to supplier resources.

You indicate that service stream acquisitions have yielded nearly 20 percent cost reduction on average to date and that the acquisition process has been greatly simplified. The suppliers help you use their products and services more effectively with innovative leaps to different and better solutions. Some of these suppliers have become strategically important to your business and now are foundations for new or expanded services you offer.

You suggest specific areas of focus based on your own business success, which you detail:

Food Service

- Consolidated supply base from three suppliers to one, creating an 18 percent acquisition cost reduction.
- Eliminated duplicate management.
- Manage traffic and consumption with supplier data.
- Provide consistent service across the country.
- Conduct a quality/customer satisfaction program.
- Review improvement plans quarterly.

Office Products

- Consolidated supply base from six suppliers to one, creating 36 percent acquisition cost reduction.
- Offer desktop delivery.

- Offer broader scope of services.
- Have joint productivity improvement goal with supplier.
- Have only one point of information management.
- Provide consistent products and support nation-wide.
- Have improved distribution methods.

Forms Management

- Consolidate supply base from five suppliers to one, achieving a 15 percent acquisition cost reduction.
- Provide closed warehouse.
- Provide on-site store front presence.
- Give supplier incentive to improve usage and reduce cost year after year.
- Discover innovation in electronic forms through continual improvement.

Although your visitors' inquiries regarded purchases of indirect materials and services, you can't resist providing some direct materials results.

Raw Materials

- Consolidated supply base from 5,500 suppliers to 1,500; on the way to 350.
- Converted scheduling from the push of material requirements planning (MRP) to demand pull.
- Colocated supply teams with design engineering, resulting in supplier involvement eleven months earlier in those areas.
- Improved quality levels dramatically.
- Cut administrative work in half.

You summarize by highlighting that your early efforts yielded better suppliers, better costs, better capability, and better support for your company's goals and that although you are a long way from completion you have attracted a lot of attention and achieved solid results.

Your visitors are impressed and wonder aloud how quickly they can begin to implement some of these ideas. You conclude by inviting them to a supply management workshop for new suppliers in which you and other supply leaders will help them to develop a specific plan of action.

As you bid your guests good-bye, you realize you are almost late to the Consumer Products and Systems Business Sourcing Council Meeting. You are scheduled to review the effectiveness of last quarter's purchasing expenditures program and outline a critical path of change for the remainder of the year. Following this session, you will meet with the leading marketing directors to finalize details for the Supplier Innovation Conference next month. Key core suppliers of equipment, chemicals, information systems, and medical technology will assemble to create the next generation of therapeutic product and service innovation concepts. Seven supplier teams and your marketing, technical, and supply management leaders will work together in a two-day workshop to define new dimensions of what is possible and in what time frames.

As the day draws to a close, you have two more stops to make, the first to meet the communication team made up of supply managers from various locations and businesses. In this session you review the effectiveness of the previous year's communication efforts and discuss progress in changing usage techniques and improving the supply process. The session outcomes will be used to create next year's communication plan spanning all business locations, including the roles for senior business executives.

Finally, you return to your office to meet with your immediate staff, a group of supply leaders responsible for the purchases of the total business. In this session you and your supply leaders recap the effectiveness of the supply management program and review the standard measurement process for the upcoming year. This measurement process will be communicated to all supply managers and business and manufacturing leaders. As you look at the results you have all achieved in two short years, you are struck by the magnitude of change: large decreases in expenditures, completely new acquisition processes, a remarkably smaller supplier base, totally integrated business and supply management work teams, functioning organizational mechanisms for reviewing supply management results and priorities, supplier involvement in critical development work, and, best of all, a new base of skills you would not have thought possible in this short period of time.

And yet you remember the keys were remarkably simple: three core processes, market analysis, and benchmarking. Your supply leaders created whole new strategies for almost every purchase stream by applying these concepts and processes consistently.

Just before you leave, the telephone rings to reward you with one last opportunity to implement the supply management process in a recently acquired company. Oh, and the company would like an estimate of the first year's benefits. (Some things don't change.)

Having given you a glimpse of the future, let us hasten to remind you that this entire implementation process is a journey, composed of many steps and side trips. The most courageous move of all is to take the first step, for as the ancient Chinese proverb says, The longest journey begins with a single step. Here are several steps to get you started:

- Consolidate suppliers for one supply stream.
- Form a team to benchmark other companies' procurement practices.
- Meet with the senior leaders of a key supplier and discuss your futures.
- Conduct a market/industry analysis on your most important raw material or service.
- Classify your large purchases into core and non-core groups.
- Invite procurement employees to describe their knowledge of leading practices and opportunities.

Remember, whatever you do does not need to be perfect the first time out. It is more important that some step be taken, some action completed.

Several years ago we met with the chairman of a major multibillion-dollar corporation shortly after we helped the organization to implement the supply management process. The purpose of our meeting was to share our learning and observations for future work. The chairman asked how we would compare this implementation process to other major projects in which we had been involved. We said, "Every business faces some really hard challenges: the need to secure market share by actually changing customers' buying and usage behavior, the need to invent the next-generation technology in order to retain market leadership, the need to streamline manufacturing or major processing centers to keep costs low. These challenges require the full focus of an organization in order to conquer not only internal problems and barriers but also external conflicts of unknown proportions. These challenges are truly difficult. The leadership challenge here is to provide the focus and energy necessary to rally the entire organization in concert, to assemble the right blend of skills, and to spark the essential flash of creativity and innovation necessary to develop special solutions that are uniquely yours."

On the other hand, supply management implementation is *not* hard. It *is* complex—lots of suppliers, lots of purchases, too many internal demands—but it's not hard in the sense that you need to invent new solutions or technologies to succeed. The leadership challenge here is to adopt leading-edge strategies and practices for all purchase streams.

The purchase streams are known, the suppliers are generally known, and the suppliers are ready and waiting to engage with their knowledge of technology, new processes, and best practices. The steps to put it together are simple, the implementation guidelines are straightforward and few. The greatest challenge is to create a critical mass of supply leaders who are willing to overcome the inertia of the status quo, the stagnation of disinterest, and often belligerent demands of personal choice. This handful of dragon-slaying supply leaders, given a set of tools, a blueprint, and committed leadership, will simply hammer away until it's done.

IMPLEMENTATION GUIDE

Well, that's it, folks. So, what are you going to do now?

- Continue to admire the problem?
- Leave this book on your shelf for a rainy-day staff project?
- Buck it to a subordinate with an "FYI"?
- Let your competitors implement these ideas first?
- Review the book's Implementation Guide sections to develop a plan of action? (Getting warmer.)
- Leave your office and visit a supply manager, buyer, or somebody in procurement? (Not bad—not bad!)
- Create a forum of senior peers to lead the new supply management process? (By Jove, we think you've got it!)

You have now invested some direct and indirect costs (this book's price and your time to read it). You have gained insight that, if available, would cost a great deal in consulting time. Realize your return on the investment. Whatever you do, take the action. Provide the leadership—and do it before the opportunity goes to someone else.

Enjoy the journey!

Index

Standard Industrial
    Classification (SIC) Code,
    190
standard purchases
    core, 123, 136–137
    non-core, 122, 134–136
    of products vs. services, 127
strategic procurement, 99
suppliers
    annual meetings of, 215–216
    community of, 88–91
    consolidation of, 26, 115
    input of, in engineering
        process, 37
    with most competitive
        advantage, 59–60
    proliferation of, 11–13
    roundtables of, 217
    value chain mapping done
        by, 73
    workshops involving,
        217–219
supply chains, 24, 26, 40
supply management
    benefits of, 85–88
    competitive advantage from,
        52
    and continual improvement
        process, 81–82
    core processes of, 55–58,
        78–79, 96
    and decentralization, 50
    definitions of, 4–5, 49–50
    focus of, 50, 51
    as idea, 5–6
    implementing, *see*
        implementing supply
        management
    and market/industry
        analysis, 59–68
    as "outside-in process," 50

and scoping analysis,
    82–83
skill set for, 85
as strategic management
    process, 52–53
and total cost of ownership,
    75–78
traditional procurement
    processes vs., 50
and utility/functionality of
    supply streams, 53–55
and value chain mapping,
    68–75
supply management leadership
    forums, 174–175
supply managers, 50, 52
supply networks, 38–42,
    148–149
supply stream(s), 24–26, 35,
    44–46, 114–144
    classification of, 117–119, 124
    core customized purchases in,
        121, 133–134
    core standard purchases in,
        123, 136–137
    and implementation of
        supply management, 58
    and leadership, 147–148
    management strategies for,
        117–118, 127–131
    measuring effectiveness of,
        183–193
    models of, 213–214
    non-core customized
        purchases in, 120, 131–133
    non-core standard purchases
        in, 122, 134–136
    and reengineering, 138–142
    strategy implications of
        various types of, 124–127
    utility/functionality of, 53–55

supply teams, 226
support, from supply
management organization,
167–168
supporting technologies, 37–38,
40, 42, 43

task analysis, management, 16
TCO, *see* total cost of ownership
teams, 57–58, 226
technology life cycle, 129
time
and communication of
"mental shifts," 211–212
as competitive advantage,
34–35
lack of, as barrier to change,
109–110, 112
time-to-market cycle, 35–37
definition of, 22–23
titanium dioxide (case study),
27–30
total cost of ownership (TCO),
75–78, 114, 210
as effectiveness measurement,
185–186, 188

and scoping analysis, 82–83
summary of, 95
traditional procurement
process, supply
management vs., 50
transaction frequency, and
purchase cost, 139–142
turf protectionism, 108–109, 112
turnkey supplier strategies,
134–136

value chain maps/mapping,
68–75, 139
benefits of using, 70–71
completing, 73–75
creating, 71
definition of, 70
steps in, 68–70
summary of, 94
types of work in, 71–72
virtual corporations, 37–38

work flow, material/service, 54
workshops, 156, 174, 217–219

Xerox, 100, 132